The Good Stuff

Oldmansailing

The Good Stuff

Book One

by John Passmore

Samsara Press

Samsara Press

First published 2022

© John Passmore

John Passmore has asserted his right under the Copyright, Designs and Patents Act of 1988 to be identified as the Author of this work.

All rights reserved. No part of this publication may be reproduced or transmitted in any form or by any means, electronic or mechanical, including photocopying, recording, or any information storage or retrieval system without prior permission from the Author.

No responsibility for loss caused to any individual or organisation acting on or refraining from action as a result of the material in this publication can be accepted by the Author.

ISBN: 9798816009430

Cover design by **www.BeyondBookCovers.com**
Cover photo: The Skelligs by John Passmore

Dedication

George Passmore
1916 – 2000

My father taught me to sail.

He taught himself to sail too - at the age of 14. He didn't know what the shrouds were for, so he tied them in a bundle at the bottom of the mast.

The mast fell down.

He owned a succession of boats after that. One of them, Wanderer, he bought off Eric Hiscock (who went on to write the seminal Around the World in Wanderer III). Years later, they met at the Boat Show, and Father reminded him.

"Ah yes," said Hiscock. "Pig of a boat, wasn't she?"

In these pages, you will see just how much of an influence Father had on my sailing.

It is time to say thank you.

Grab a chance and you won't be
sorry for a might-have-been.

- The words of Arthur Ransome carved into the bulkhead of Wanderer III when Eric and Susan Hiscock set off on their circumnavigation in 1952.

Contents

Introduction i
1 The Black Box 1
2 Disaster Management The Cooker 6
3 Not the Fastnet 12
4 Hats, Turnips and Geraniums 17
5 The Three-Year Itch 25
6 The OSTAR 30
7 Largo's OSTAR 41
8. Real Men Don't Use Spinnaker Squeezers 49
9 Frank Sinatra and the Left-Flanking Movement 54
10 The Anchor and How to Survive It 59
11 Going Slowly 66
12 Wash Day Blues 68
13 Bright Eyes? 70
14 Seadog Trials 71
15 Bumps In the Night 73
16 The Jet Skier Solution 76
17 Jimmy the One 79
18 Tacking the Dog 82
19 The Staff of Life 85
20 Boat Time 88
21 Beware the Singlehander 90
22 Doggone! 93
23 Sorry, Officer, I'm Sinking 96
24 Is There Anybody There? 98
25 Two's Company 101
26 One Careful Owner 104
27 Beyond the Pale 107
28 Tackling Everest 110
29 Marked for Life 113
30 Holland Revisited 116
31 Space Craft 121
32 It's a Seadog's Life 124
33 Pan-Pan Medico 127

- 34 All Aboard for a New Life 130
- 35 The Next Step 134
- 36 Horsey Island 137
- 37 Watts, Amps, and Angst 140
- 38 The Pint Pot 143
- 39 Woodbridge 146
- 40 Hot Gossip 150
- 41 Kent 153
- 42 An Inspector Calls 156
- 43 Walking the Plank 159
- 44 Holidays 162
- 44 Life of Luxury 165
- 45 Beaulieu 168
- 47 Mud, Glorious Mud 171
- 48 Cornwall 174
- 49 Shower Power 176
- 50 Watchet 179
- 51 Mumbles 181
- 52 Flying the Flag 184
- 53 Swansea 187
- Books by the Same Author Also Available from Amazon 190
- About the Author 192

Introduction

I am writing this in the North Atlantic, about a third of the way between Mindelo in the Cape Verde Islands and Grenada in the Caribbean. It is a typical trade wind crossing: The sun is shining, the breeze is dead astern at about 18 knots, and *Samsara*, under twin headsails, is looking after herself as she has for the past week while reeling off 100-120 miles a day.

With 1487 still to go, it will take another ten days at least – probably closer to two weeks. It is my first trade-wind crossing – a rite of passage. I have been looking forward to this. I have been imagining this all my life.

Twenty-eight years ago, I thought it was ready to go. I gave up my career as a newspaper correspondent and announced that I was going sailing. When I went into the *Evening* Standard office for the last time, two librarians came down to the editorial floor bearing armfuls of wire trays loaded with buff folders.

These were the "Corres files" – everything this particular correspondent had written for any of the group's titles since he arrived as a keen young reporter doing his first night shift at the *Daily Mail* in 1976 – in other words, 20 years' worth of work, near enough.

My colleagues gathered around and picked over the archive: There were despatches here from China and Czechoslovakia, from Berlin and Bognor.

With a flourish, I emptied the whole lot into the wastepaper bin. "Not wanted on voyage."

The News Editor, a great friend and mentor, began pulling them out, stacking them neatly again: "You can't throw this away! This is a lifetime's work! This is history!"

It was true. If I had been an outgoing Prime Minister, it would have been stored under environmentally-controlled conditions at my old university college, available to historians as "The Passmore Archive".

But then, I was not a Prime Minister and never went to university. I put them back in the bin.

In the end, we compromised, and I kept two folders. These

covered the end of the Cold War and the fall of the Berlin Wall, including the drive I took with all the East Germans in their 2-stroke *Trabbis* as they escaped down through Czechoslovakia and Austria into West Germany.

There, we plunged into the biggest party I have ever witnessed as people were reunited with parents and siblings and ex-spouses and, absurdly, had bananas pressed on them at every turn. The *Wessies* were convinced that the *Ossies* had never seen a banana.

I have those two folders still - and the centre spread from Tiananmen Square. My children find them interesting, sometimes.

But there was another archive that did get preserved – virtually intact. Once I had my feet under the table at the Daily Mail, I bought a small boat – an 18ft Caprice called *Amicus* – and started reading magazines such as *Yachting Monthly* and *Practical Boat Owner*. Since I spent my working days writing for newspapers, it made sense in the evenings to submit the occasional piece to the magazines.

They seemed to like what I sent them, and this became a regular thing. In particular, Andrew Bray, the editor of *Yachting Monthly*, was happy to print whatever I offered him – even my attempts at cartoons. After the first few years, I was being published so frequently that it seemed a good idea to file these as well – by tossing them into a bottom drawer and forgetting about them.

They spent years in that bottom drawer – and then more years in Tamsin's parents' attic. My mother added to them. So did my sister - and the newsdesk assistant at the Evening Standard. Bit by bit, the excavated pages, the fading photocopies and occasional complete publication grew into a collection spanning, as far as I can make out, the years 1985 – 2003.

That was when I moved ashore and, as described in the Old Man Sailing book, attempted to settle down and be content in a small market town, looking at boats while walking the dog along the river and trying to race a Laser round the buoys on a Saturday.

Now that I am living aboard once more, it has all started up again – but instead of submitting hard copy in envelopes – or latterly trailing all round town trying to find a fax machine, I have my own blog at the end of a data signal – and with it, the wonderful sensation of being in direct contact with the readers. After all, they respond instantly as if we are old friends (which I like to think we are).

So, it was on a whim – as blithely as I had thrown away the newspaper cuttings – that I rescued the sailing archive, scooping it up on a visit home before setting out from Weymouth. Then it spent six months stuffed into the bookcase between *Caribbean Passage-Making* and *The Atlantic Islands Pilot*.

It was only after the first 500 miles of the crossing to the West Indies, realising there really was very little to do but sit in the sun, that I cast around for something new to read. That was when I pulled out the folder from the bookcase. Immediately, all those pages spilled out all over the cabin. There was stuff in there I had forgotten all about: pieces I had written for the Ocean Cruising Club's *Flying Fish* magazine, my "award-winning" entries in the Rival Owners Association Newsletter.

There was *Dogwatch,* the column Andrew Bray gave me when he moved from Yachting Monthly to Yachting World: I remember him telling me I could write about anything I liked as long as it had something to do with boats and would make people smile. Had any writer ever been given a broader brief? *Dogwatch* ran for a decade, every month from 1993 to 2003 – a book all by itself. I wrote about everything you can imagine (and some things you might not): dockside hosepipes, marina showers, knickers…

At one point, I enclosed a note with the monthly fax, asking if it wasn't all getting a bit absurd. Was this really what he wanted? Andrew sent back: "Keep it up. It's good stuff."

Dogwatch only came to an end when I had been living in a house for three years and sat up late one night leaning hard against the deadline and typed onto the blank screen: "I've had enough of this…"

You can find that final despatch on the last page of Book Two – but, in case you don't have it yet, here is an extract: *I've been doing this column since April 1993. That's more than ten years, 130 columns and 100,000 words. It's a blockbuster novel.*

I have, in my time, discussed ensigns, toothache and gangplanks. I have considered the merits of jetskis (and found none). I extolled the virtues of a dressing gown aboard a boat and established the principles of navigation by smell – and where would we be without Passmore's Law of Lost Hats or my definitive guide to the yacht club showers of the UK?

Then there was the dog, remember the dog? Remember his ladder-climbing prowess and midnight leaps onto his bunk (somehow forgetting that someone else had borrowed it for the night.)

It's all here in what I call the Dogwatch Catalogue – a list of topics that I started keeping when I realised there was a very real danger of repeating myself. Mind you; there were occasions when I ignored the list and decided the story was too good to be limited to one outing – like five of us in a Folkboat back in the Fifties with my sister sleeping on the floor – and the way Father would rise to check the warps at 0300 and step straight onto her face.

There was Bridgemanship and the herrings down the back of the cooker in Amsterdam – the party we had in the middle of the OSTAR with half a dozen of us meeting up in the middle of the Atlantic on 4143.5MHz for champagne and canapés. And, gracious me, did I really say that about the Woodbridge harbour master? How did I know I was going to go back there and buy a house?

Then there was the Daily Telegraph: Max Hastings had tried to recruit me from the Mail when he took over as editor in 1986. When I resigned in 1995, I went back to him and suggested a column. We agreed that I would write about a voyage around the UK coastline – he had enough about palm trees. It ended up as a personal journey into small-scale family life.

The Mail's "You" magazine gave me space - and the local paper, the East Anglian Daily Times. Also, for some reason, I have never been able to explain, Australian Women's Weekly.

Spreading it out all over the rolling cabin as we surfed ever westwards, I sifted through accounts of the Mother of All Broaches off the Grand Banks, levitating the dog at Rye, getting marooned in the mud at Mersea Island...

There was the original piece from the front page of the Telegraph's Weekend section explaining that Tamsin and I were giving up everything to embark on a new and better life. The whole story of that life slid off my lap onto the cabin sole, unfolding month by month in delicate, yellowing newsprint: Remember that walk across the blazing sands of St Aubyn's Bay and deciding there was room on the boat for a baby? The search for lunch in Milford Haven - ante-natal care above a sex shop in Amsterdam - putting down roots for a winter in a cottage ashore – and then the wrench in tearing them up to set off again?

And, of course, the final, awful discovery amongst the First War cemeteries of Picardy that if one baby on a small boat was hard work, two was a recipe for broken dreams…

This wasn't just good stuff. This was mesmerising - a life in snapshots, following the undercurrents as the narrative unfolded a fortnight at a time.

Some of it fills in the gaps in the Old Man Sailing book. Some of it seems to come from another life entirely.

Not everything is included: For one thing, I didn't start collecting cuttings until 1985, and I have left out anything that didn't seem relevant to the story. *The Law of Lost Hats* is missing because that was included in the original book – and, of course, the capsize of *Lottie Warren* and my rescue by helicopter was done to death (almost literally) and got a whole chapter to itself.

The humour of Dogwatch is juxtaposed with the sometimes darker passages from the newspapers – the squalor, the arguments (the salt cellar is thrown across the cabin – a small boy forces himself between us: "Stop shouting, stop shouting!") But was there any point in writing any of it unless it was real?

In putting it all together, I will admit to a weakness for tinkering with the copy until - as used to happen -the editor tears it out of the typewriter. So there has been much editing and complete re-writes for no better reason than I felt I could do better. Lacking any sense of shame, I have left in my own shortcomings and even corrected attempts to portray events in a better light than they deserved – as I said, I am not an out-going prime minister…

** Photographs and a glossary of nautical terms can be found on my blog at www.oldmansailing.com.
J.P.

Chapter 1
The Black Box

Halfway between Guernsey and Lésardrieux, just by that ominous legend on the chart about "magnetic anomalies", the gremlins got into the VHF.

Well, it seemed more likely than the other explanation – that Jersey Radio had left the set switched to *one watt*. But certainly, all they seemed able to offer was a long, if dignified, silence.

This was broken by another plaintive call from a second confused yachtsman, also twiddling knobs and getting nowhere. So I called him up.

"I can't raise them either," I complained. "I ought to be able to. I'm halfway between Guernsey and Lésardrieux. Where are you?"

That was when the only other person in the world I could talk to told me this: "Where am I? I'm… hold on a minute… I'm at 48 degrees 75.31'N; 03 degrees 26.25'W°"

The Decca Navigator had struck again! The conversation progressed a little beyond that, and we established that he had just come out of Lésardrieux bound West. But somehow, he couldn't bring himself to put it so simply.

Like many of the new generation of button-pushing yachtsmen, he was entirely obsessed with the microchips. It was a bit like asking the time of someone with a digital watch and being told "15:49" instead of ten to four.

I consoled myself with a beer and the knowledge that, according to my trusty Seafix, I was somewhere in a cocked hat ten miles by fifteen just west of the *Banc de Langoustiers.*

What worried me more was where we are going in this pastime that is supposed to get us back to nature "at one with the universe" and all that. What of the old seamanlike skills - gauging the leeway by squinting down the logline - adding a bit to the tidal stream at the end of a gale? What hope for them in an age when the black box on the bulkhead can tell you the difference between the two sides of the pencil line on the chart?

I was beginning to sound depressingly like the old boy in the yacht club who greeted the appearance of the first depth recorder back in the '50s with the question: "What happens when it goes wrong?"

And then something very embarrassing happened: My colleague and occasional crew, the somewhat dangerous Woodgates, came up with the idea of racing. Racing would test us, he expounded in the pub after work. Racing would bring us glory, he insisted, pushing another pint of Brakespear's into my hand. Against all wisdom and common sense, I entered us for the first Yachting Monthly Triangle race, described, as far as I remember, as "reasonably testing for two-handed amateur crews."

With a course centred in the Western approaches, taking in Falmouth, Crosshaven and Morgat, I could see why they would say that.

Never mind. Woodgates had a secret weapon. Unzipping his enormous sailing bag covered in yachtie logos, he produced from the mess of dank oilies and mismatched socks, the Very Latest Thing: A Decca Navigator. With the same sort of expansive promises that had got me into the race, he had talked it out of the manufacturers. We could keep it for the whole summer, he said. It would win us the race, he said.

But I wasn't going to let it run the ship – oh no! I regarded *Largo*, a Rival 32, as a "proper ship" and "proper ships", unlike modern, light displacement rubbish, don't rely on microchips.

So, we set off from Poole, bound westwards for Falmouth. It was the same as always, an ingenious plan for catching the tide off the headlands and letting the east-going stream waste itself in the bays (a plan that promptly got blown apart by a healthy westerly sending us bashing out into the Channel.) By mid-afternoon the little crosses of the dead reckoning were marching off somewhere in the direction of Ushant.

The Decca Navigator looked down from the bulkhead, beeping as it saw fit and occasionally changed one figure on its screen for another. It didn't matter to me what it changed them to; I knew where I was. Hadn't I just squinted down the log line, spent long minutes watching the compass to gauge an average of our course?

Still, it would be interesting to test the accuracy of this box of tricks.

The cross it provided (an unusual vertical and horizontal affair like something out of a maths textbook rather than the normal "X" of a DR) was some eight miles to the northeast – and only five hours after losing sight of the coast…

Thank heavens I was only borrowing the thing. Imagine spending close on a thousand quid on something that puts you eight miles out after only five hours. That's almost a mile and a half of error for every hour! By the time it got to Falmouth, it would probably think it was in the Skagerak.

It was at this point that Woodgates said something rather disrespectful and possibly mutinous: "Perhaps the machine's right, and your DR is wrong."

Well, hardly likely was it? Not when you had a skipper so steeped in the lore of the sea that his Breton cap – were it possible to prise it off his head – would keep a marine biologist entertained for a week.

But the challenge had been made. Honour was at stake. I took the trusty Seafix from its bracket. I waved it in the direction of such places as Portland Bill, the Channel Light Vessel and the Casquets.

Portland Bill was rather a long way away and had to be discounted as unreliable – after all, its bearing went with absurd accuracy straight through the middle of the Decca cross.

It was the other two which were more embarrassing. They met in a mocking fix even further to the east.

After that, I took to putting the chart away between the hourly plots. Apart from anything else, it left the table clear for ever more detailed calculation of the tides. But all the same, the two lines of crosses stalked off in two very obviously different directions down the channel.

The hand bearing compass and the beam of Channel Light Vessel joined the Seafix in siding with the Decca. The following day, even the sun agreed with the microchips. Either that or I'd done something unnatural with my transit.

It was a rather subdued skipper who sailed into Falmouth. The Decca beeped triumphantly, and Woodgates reminded me I owed him a pint of St Austell in The Chain Locker - something to do with a bet about which I could remember nothing.

Mellowed slightly later that night, I did concede that it was convenient to have an accurate fix far from land. Convenient, though hardly *important* because the old ways would always get you home in the end.

And so we progressed to Ireland and Brittany, and the crosses on the chart changed from "X" to "+" and I would nod knowledgeably over each one and say things like: "We're making a little more leeway – you can tell that by looking at the logline." Or: "A little more tide this morning – that's to be expected after that blow last night…"

And the Decca would beep in agreement – until I found the chapter in the instruction manual that tells you how to stop it. Apart from anything else, it gave me a chance to say I might get my own one day – when they come down in price, of course. After all, it was nice to have – but hardly *essential*…

In fact, it wasn't until the second half of August that I stopped being rude about the black box on the bulkhead. We had left Dixcart Bay on the east coast of Sark early in the morning so as to catch the tide up to Alderney. There was not a breath of wind, but the Channel Islands weather forecast said the visibility would improve. It seemed reasonable. Another hot day would soon burn off the mist. Even if it didn't, we could see for the best part of a mile.

But it did seem slow in clearing. We left Sark behind in the murk. With a three-and-a-half-knot tide under us, that didn't take long.

By mid-morning, we didn't have mist, we had fog: the thick, clinging kind, full of echoes and shadows of supertankers head on – the really nasty kind.

Also, we were off the southwest corner of Alderney, had only two hours of tide left and not an awfully long time to make a decision. We couldn't stay where we were with rocks on all sides and the tide ready to sweep us back to Sark. The sensible thing to do was get away to the west – under the Casquets – and come in from the North. But with another full west-going tide to come, that would take eight hours. Eight hours of swanning about in fog right on top of the Traffic Separation Scheme.

So that was how we came to navigate the Swinge without seeing either side. The channel is barely more than half a mile wide, bordered by rocks, and the book says it should not be entered in anything other than "reasonable visibility and fair weather".

But in we plunged: those vertical crosses carefully skirting the dangers., a liquid crystal pointing the way: left a bit, right a bit. The printed circuit board, full off confidence.

The first thing we saw was the breakwater at about 30 yards. It never looked so good.

It was only later, recounting the tale in The Divers, that I happened to mention we'd waited for the tide to ease off and came up slowly and cautiously.

"How slowly," they asked. "A couple of knots?"

"Something like that" I told them. "About 1.8 actually."

———

Chapter 2
Disaster Management: The Cooker

The end came as I left the shipping lanes. Ridiculous, really: just as I should have been able to relax with a cup of coffee, suddenly the boat went up in flames.

Honestly, it was as sudden as that. One moment, I was warming the pot, the next, the boat was on fire. Bright blue and yellow flames spread across the cooker, licked at the curtains and fanned out across the cabin. I let out a small shriek, leapt backwards, rammed my coccyx into the bulkhead and my head into the deckhead – which, of course, was where the flames were. I could hear my hair crackling.

It's a good thing that panic doesn't last for long. Eventually, the idea of a fire extinguisher emerged through the haze: I "pulled off ring", I "held upright", I "aimed at base of fire".

In fact, I was about to "strike knob" when I realised how much of a mess this was going to make. It would take me a fortnight to get rid of the stuff – especially in the galley which, in common with all galleys, consisted mostly of inaccessible corners.

If I'd been thinking clearly, it would have occurred to me that what we had here was an over-reaction to having panicked in the first place. I was being unnaturally blasé in the face of disaster. Any minute now I'd get out the mouth organ and start playing *Abide with Me*.

But it did give me a second's pause before "striking knob hard". I looked at the flames, which by now had spread out to embrace the lockers and, at any moment, were going to turn the Fairy Liquid bottle into a piece of meaningful contemporary sculpture. I looked. I took a deep breath. I blew.

Now, I know that blowing at the flames is not a recognised course of action included in most ships' fire precautions. They may suggest "operate extinguisher" or "sound alarm" or "assemble on boat deck" (do not run). But nowhere do they say: "Take deep breath. Direct mouth at base of fire. Blow hard."

They should. It worked.

With a single puff, the fire was out. I stood and marvelled. The damage to the boat was negligible – just a slight scorching of the curtains. It was, looking back on it, a close call.

The fact is, I have a problem with cookers. With some people, it's tides: they spend long summer afternoons sitting at 50° by the side of the river feeling foolish. Others have a horror or harbours and, after bashing into a gale all night without mishap, they arrive in the calm of the morning, get themselves the wrong side of somebody's bowsprit and end up having to be rescued by the harbourmaster.

With me, it's cookers. I have trouble with sandbanks and harbourmasters as well, of course - but not on a regular basis. The cooker syndrome probably has something to do with reading somewhere that the authorities in Sweden will not allow boatbuilders to fit pressurised gas on yachts. They view the whole idea with the same distaste as the prospect of one half of the population massacring the other half by driving their Volvos on high-octane Aquavit. Obviously, there is hardly much point in saving them from themselves if all they're going to do is go down to their boats and blow themselves up.

So, when I bought little *Amicus*, the first thing I did was rip out the gas stove and replace it with an alcohol version made in Sweden and approved by all sorts of Swedish authorities.

However, this enthusiasm for safety precautions may have been invalidated somewhat by buying the cooker not just second-hand but from my mate Jimmy who was just starting out on a career selling me dodgy cookers.

"Marvellous thing," said Jimmy. "Just run it on meths – although, I'm told that in Antigua 90 proof rum is cheaper." If ever Jimmy falls on hard times, he could do worse than setting up a stall on the Mile End Road.

I did run it on meths. The smell was indescribable. Grudgingly, Jimmy admitted that sometimes it did niff a bit, but I would get used to it – anyway, what was the slight but homely odour of methylated spirit when compared to the prospect of blowing up?

Besides, he couldn't take it back now. He'd bought a new one.

I persevered. I enquired at the chandlery: "Meths?" said the salesman. "You can't run it on meths. You're supposed to use ethyl alcohol. That's what the Swedes use. I suppose you can get it in Sweden – or you could try the chemist."

I did. The chemist offered a small medicine bottle of ethanol (for external use only). Volume for volume, it was more expensive than 90 proof rum bought in London. The chemist explained that it was against the law to sell it in any other quantity in case people preferred not to use it externally but as a replacement for rum. The French, he added helpfully, had no such qualms. You could buy it anywhere in France.

And so, in Cherbourg, in a hardware store, I loaded up with ten one-litre bottles of *alcool à brûler*, which cost hardly more than paraffin, looked like white rum and burned with a slight but not unpleasant sweet perfume.

Also, it burned very readily - so that, overfilling the cooker at the end of the annual refuelling trip to Cherbourg, I had it bursting into flames as soon as I put the kettle on. Of course, as the Swedish Inspectorate of Galley Installations would say: "It is a far, far better thing to burn the ship down than to blow it up."

I got the chance to try the alternative the following year when I sold *Amicus* and bought *Largo* and inherited another gas cooker. This one lasted a couple of years before the rust triumphed over the congealed bacon fat to get at the machine's vitals. Never mind, Jimmy was swapping boats too and just happened to have a magnificent old Taylor's cooker to spare. I drove at once down to the east coast – which just shows you how the mind can play tricks on the memory.

The cooker certainly was magnificent; a veritable brass artefact with a vitreous enamel hob the colour of molten toffee. It was not, admittedly, plumbed in, so he was not able to demonstrate it. But it did have the Taylor name on a plate on the oven door – and as everyone knows, Taylor's cookers go on and on forever.

I bought it.

For the next two years, when people asked me if I had a hobby, I did not tell them I had a boat. I told them I had a paraffin cooker. This was because I never seemed to sail the boat. But I did spend long absorbing weekends taking the cooker to pieces.

The first problem was that the pressure tank did not hold pressure. You could boil a kettle by pumping all the while, but it is possible that the energy required - if applied to a generator - would have run an electric kettle and a microwave on the side. I had the pressure tank welded back together again.

Then the burners would produce only a yellow flame which covered the bottom of the pots with soot – except when the yellow flames shot all the way up to the deckhead and covered that with soot instead. I pricked the jets and got a squirt of pressurised paraffin straight in my eye.

I dismantled the jets, cleaned every part and reassembled them. This time the paraffin leaked out of the bottom in a puddle. I dismantled everything again and took the lot to the hardware shop.

The man behind the counter looked at the pieces as if they could be put together to make a Roman vase and nodded wisely. He announced: "Haven't seen one of these for a long time. That's the old model you've got there. Don't do spares for that anymore."

One of life's essential little truths began to dawn on me: What was the point of having a cooker you couldn't get spares for? I hauled out the credit card and bought all the parts necessary to upgrade the ancient Taylor's to the modern specification you could get spares for.

Another trip to the man who welded the pressure tank, another week's wait, and I had a cooker that looked exactly the same as before but was, in fact, the very latest thing in paraffin technology.

And it worked. I filled the little cups with meths. I lit it. I waited until it burned out. I opened the valve. I lit the vapour and - as if by a miracle - I was rewarded with a clear green flame.

Ah, what a moment was that. I sat and looked at it rather as James Watt must have sat and looked at his steam engine pumping away – and I said, with deep satisfaction: "It works. It actually works."

To celebrate, I made a cup of tea – without having to wipe half a pound of soot off the deckhead afterwards. Then I went off to the hardware shop to spread the good news and buy all the spares that would keep it working well into the next century.

While I was at it, I took the opportunity to buy a bottle of meths as well – at least, I started to. I got halfway through the transaction before the man standing beside me said quietly: " I wouldn't buy that if I were you. Not for a Taylor's cooker."

"No?"

"Definitely not. I had a Taylor's cooker and I used meths on it just like you and it burned with a green flame. Well, I didn't think anything of it until I had a friend aboard who was an analytical chemist, and he told me that the green flame came from the brazing burning away."

He let the significance of that sink in for a bit and then added, just in case I couldn't work it out for myself: "Once the brazing burns through, you'll get blazing paraffin spraying all over the cabin. Not very nice, that. I wouldn't buy meths if I were you."

I did not buy meths. I went straight to the phone box on the corner and called Blakes in Portsmouth. The man on the other end seemed to have had calls like this before. He began by saying "Ah," in a way that suggests that somewhere a nail has been hit on the head.

"We've had a few calls about this. It seems that some methylated spirit manufacturers are using a different process. What you want is the kind that does not say "mineralised" on the bottle – that's if you can find it. Some people have found it rather hard to come by."

That was great. So what was I supposed to do when I was unable to find this "un-mineralised" meths?

"Ah, now there I can help you. What you need is one of those butane blow torches. Just play it around the element for a minute or two and it should light straight away."

The man at Blakes really was trying to be helpful. He had no way of knowing that the whole extravagant shambles had been dedicated to getting bottled gas *off* the boat. He really was a very nice man.

Which is why *Largo* now has a gas cooker. I simply gave up. If we blow up, then I shall arrive at the Pearly Gates saying I tried. The Swedish Inspectorate of Galley Installations could have no complaints about my good intentions.

Which is why, for the first time in my life, I bought a brand new cooker. Jimmy tried to sell me his latest but at the time it came attached to a 45ft steel ketch in the Med.

With memories of the rusting monster, I had started out with in *Largo*, I went for the top of the range, a grand and shining affair called "The Atlantic" – that seemed to conjure up the right image.

However, while it certainly looked the part, I soon discovered that all that shines is not necessarily stainless steel. For instance, someone had decided to make the cooker out of the full gamut of alloys, none of which seemed to get on with any of the others. By the end of the first season, the pan clamps were welded to their screw fittings, I had to replace the rusted rivets with monel ones, and the bolt holding the grill pan together turned out to be mild steel.

I mentioned this to the salesman on the chandler's stand at the boat show. Guess what he said: "We keep asking them to upgrade their specifications, but they seem satisfied with them the way they are."

I've still got the cooker, of course. This year the jets separated into two halves, and the gas must have been escaping down into the grill because, when I went to light it, there was a "woof", and a bright blue flame took all the hairs off the back of my hand.

I should have been alarmed. I should have panicked, or at the very least, worried that you can't actually blow out a gas explosion – with gas, it's the explosion that tends to blow you out.

Instead, I just struck another match, lit everything that would light and had a cup of tea.

The plain fact is that, like the marina blunderer who must make port somehow, or the patient resident of the sandbank as he feels the keel touch once more, I had come to terms with the inevitable.

And besides, short of living on self-heating cans for the rest of my sailing days, I was running out of options.

Chapter 3
Not the Fastnet

We didn't do the Fastnet this year.

Well, considering the way things turned out, it's not surprising. With hearty ocean racers streaming into Poole swearing "Never again"; with bits falling off million-pound boats designed for Cape Horn, it wasn't really a race for cruising men looking for a bit of excitement.

Cruising men could feel proud of their common sense as they listened to the forecast offering a 50% chance of a Force 9 – and then made plans to send the week turning out the garage instead.

But cruising men who didn't even get past the first qualifying race, who retired ignominiously two months before the start – they can only blame someone else.

It really wasn't my fault, at least, not to begin with. When Woodgates first suggested it, I said "No" with all the conviction of Captain Bligh on the subject of a workers' co-operative. I mean, the Fastnet's big-league stuff – look what happened in 1979. The Fastnet is no picnic – which, of course, is precisely the attraction for Woodgates who crewed for Robin Knox-Johnson and, I suspect, has been sleeping in his Musto Ocean Racing outfit ever since.

But *Largo* is no *British Airways* – and while she's capable of completing the Fastnet, we would likely arrive in Plymouth when all the parties were over, which is hardly the object of the exercise. It was a wonderful idea, but not really practical.

The trouble with ideas like that is that, once they become practical, they're very difficult to discard – like, for instance, when we were offered the loan of an Offshore One Design 34, a boat of such staggering performance that Woodgates, lying awake at nights in his Mustos, started rehearsing victory speeches.

From that point on, there really was no hope for us.

I wrote to the Royal Ocean Racing Club. I outlined in modest terms our enormous experience and suggested that we might be allowed to compete after doing only one qualifying race instead of two.

The man from RORC wrote back. He could see how highly experienced we were, but rules were rules. So we picked out a couple of races from the programme, and I made my next appalling error of judgement.

"We'll need a couple of extra bods," I said.

"We'll need a crew of seven," said Woodgates.

Seven! On a 34ft boat? Where would we put them all? What would they do? With two of us on the Triangle Race, I had occasionally found the boat rather crowded. The year before that, I went to Spain all on my own – which really is the only way to keep the companionway clear.

The idea of seven really didn't bear thinking about.

Woodgates was adamant. He produced a foredeck hand with experience on OODs – who could be relied on to insist that nine would not be too many.

We compromised. This was, after all, only the first qualifying race – just a quick spin down to Portland and back. It wasn't as if we were going to have to organise watches and what have you.

So there would be four of us. As well as me and Woodgates, we would be joined by Bill Cross who has a Moody 29 and the sort of competitive instinct that makes him worry about the performance of his furling genny.

And there would be Dick Durham. Normally Dick would not dream of being seen on anything built after 1930, but someone had told him about the parties.

Everything was organised. We would pick up the boat on the Thursday morning and have two full days to get used to her before the start.

Somehow, I had the idea that those two days would be filled with relentless spinnaker drills. I had this notion that hundreds of square feet of nylon would be shooting up and down the mast like Nelson's signal flags. I had visions of us gybing it down the length of the Solent until the manoeuvre went off with the kind of wordless efficiency I always imagine you find on Admiral's Cup boats.

I was wrong again. First, I got stuck in Belgium on a story – which at least offered the interesting diversion of seeing my work disrupt my sailing rather than the other way round – and then the boat wasn't ready.

The wonderful, high-performance racer which was going to whisk us to victory was still ashore, without its mast and all our plans - not to mention Woodgates' speech – looked like coming to nothing.

Quite what happened over the next 24 hours, I was never quite sure. I do remember stuffing foreign coins into foreign telephone boxes, only to hear Woodgates shouting: "Don't worry, everything's going to be fine."

Usually, he says this shortly before disaster strikes.

The owner of the mastless, land-bound racer said: "Don't worry, everything's going to be fine." He'd arranged for us to borrow another OOD. We picked it up on the Friday at lunchtime.

It wasn't our fault that the start was on Saturday morning. But perhaps we should have realised what it means to sail a proper racing boat.

It had nine winches. What can anyone possibly want with nine winches?

Woodgates suggested that was one for each member of the crew – but since there had been some confusion over the arrangements and Durham was at that moment pottering about on his floating antique in Leigh-on-Sea, we had three winches a piece.

Somehow, relentless spinnaker drills didn't seem so important to a crew who had never in their lives reefed without benefit of a topping lift ... who were completely taken by surprise when the mainsail came down and promptly fell over the side instead of staying obediently in its track ... and what can you say about three full-grown men standing on the foredeck, discussing what the adjustable baby stay might be for.

But what we lacked in expertise, we made up in confidence. In Cowes, we tied up alongside another OOD – with nine people standing on each other's toes, politely waiting their turn at the companionway.

"You'll be working hard," said the skipper, squinting down the hatch and assuming we must have some more down there somewhere.

"No problem," I said. "We'll just take it slowly. It's not as if we need to win."

And then we went off to dinner at Murrays where we covered the table with entry forms which invited us to describe how we intended to cut loose the rig in the event of a dismasting – and then asked: "Are you sure?"

Believe me, we weren't sure of anything. Probably, out of the lot of us, I was the most confused. I'd never sailed a strange boat in my life. I hadn't even taken one of those bareboat charters in the Mediterranean, the ones with lissom creatures are fixed to the foredeck like the anchor in chocks. No, I was having trouble. Mostly, I was having trouble with the loo.

Now, I'm something of an expert on marine plumbing. If there was a national championship for retrieving small change from round the bend, I'd be up there collecting the gold medal. But I had never attacked a Lavac before – and the prospect of starting a race without at least persuading it to dispose of its contents didn't bear thinking about.

"Do you know how to get at the pump?" I asked the skipper of eight on the boat next door.

He had no idea. His loo was serviced by the yard, he said – which, I suppose, is the difference between racing and cruising skippers.

Then Bill discovered the sight gauge on the fuel tank. We'd been looking for this ever since we ran out of water and wondered if there really was "plenty in the tanks".

There wasn't. Or at least, the sight gauge was empty.

The start was at 0930. The fuelling berth opened at 0900. We were still pulling up sails at the ten-minute gun.

In fact, what with one thing and another, we never did go through the identification gate. I remember seeing a distinguished-looking old gentleman in a blazer and club tie sitting in a motorboat looking the other way – but I seemed to have other things on my mind at the time.

One of these was the peculiar habit racing boats have of turning round the moment you let go of the tiller. On *Largo,* you can let go of the tiller, take a walk around the deck, and still find her pointing in the same direction when you get back.

It had simply never occurred to me that in proper racing boats, the helmsman is not supposed to let go of the tiller, let alone join in the hunt for the main halyard. Suddenly a crew of three didn't seem so many after all.

It was a wonder, really, that we started at all. But when the gun went, there we were in the middle of everything with spinnakers cracking all around us - while we waited for all the fuss to die down before setting our own.

It was sensible: strange boat, small crew – and anyway, it wasn't as if we were trying to win.

The Owner, appearing in a speedboat off Lymington, seemed not to appreciate this. He made the sort of gestures racing yachtsmen make to each other, but the only effect of this was that the spinnaker wrapped itself round the forestay.

It was all turning into a disaster. We ripped the spinnaker, missed the tide and even Woodgates - who had long since abandoned his speech – suggested this was all getting rather silly.

That night, as the rest of the fleet charged up and down the Channel, we sat in the Pier View's restaurant holding a morose postmortem.

I distinctly remember saying I was a rotten skipper. I lacked the quality of leadership, I said – even at school, they'd never made me a prefect. Woodgates blamed the six missing crew who could have had a winch apiece and spent many happy hours unwrapping spinnakers. And Bill blamed the strange boat. As he said: "By the time we got back to Cowes, we were actually making her go rather fast."

He was right, of course – and the man at RORC was right when he insisted on two qualifying races.

The fact is that it doesn't matter how many exotic pilot books you have above the chart table or how many famous names you can drop.

What makes the difference between the competent racing crew and those who really shouldn't be allowed near the start are the things that we all take for granted on our own boats – like how to get the plumbing apart and whether you've got a topping lift.

The Good Stuff – Book One

Chapter 4
Hats, Turnips and Geraniums

There is a little-known law of physics which states that the wind, acting on a peaked cap, shall increase by the square of the speed at which the wearer makes a grab for it.

It is called Passmore's First Law of Lost Hats and it came into play 400 miles southwest of Ushant during the 1987 Henri Lloyd Azores and Back Race.

The sponsor gets a mention there because it was the sponsor's hat – or, to be more precise, a sun visor with Henri-Lloyd Active sportswear written on it and a blue plastic peak so enormous that it had to be gybed with both hands in anything more than a Force 2. But it did have one very practical use. It was ideal for keeping spray off the spectacles as I lay on the windward deck reading Frederick Forsyth.

Quite what I was doing lying in the sun reading thrillers in the middle of a race is something the competition with their water ballast and running backstays found difficult to understand. But *Largo* is a Rival 32 and different values apply – rather as they did when the sun visor leapt nimbly over the side.

I went back for it.

Well, I'd become very attached to it, and obviously, it wasn't going to sink - and anyway, how was I to know it would keep slipping off the boathook, and I'd have to have three goes at picking it up? People don't appreciate the problems we singlehanded racing sailors have to face.

There's a similarly good explanation for the reason I turned round after three days and started sailing back towards the start. This time it was Mrs Thatcher's fault.

I had been listening to her on Radio Four's final Election Call – and great fun it was too, being little more than institutionalised heckling. I hardly noticed the invective fading as the battery died.

Normally, of course, I would have switched over, started the engine and charged up both batteries. But then, of course, I wouldn't have been able to hear how Sir Robin Day dealt with the man from

Macclesfield who had such strong views on the economy. Besides, the little car radio/cassette player hardly used much electricity.

How was I supposed to know I'd left the navigation lights on, and the engine inspection light – and the compass light as well?

By the time Mrs T had sorted out unemployment, the bomb, inner cities and privatisation, and I turned the key, I was rewarded with a soft "click" from the starter motor – and then nothing.

But did I curse and fret? Did I face the prospect of 900 miles with no electricity? Not a bit of it. I was prepared. I had a wind generator. I looked up to the top of the pole where it turned lethargically in an apparent wind reduced almost to nothing by *Largo's* four knots to the southwest. I could count the blades as they went round. The batteries weren't getting so much as a milliamp. Never mind. The wind would change.

The wind had better change. I didn't want to miss the results the following night.

But at 1700 the next day, the wind was Force 3 from the north, and not only was I facing the prospect of a second night of hanging a hurricane lamp in the rigging and yawning a lot - but there would be no election results unless I fancied the prospect of spending the night plugged into the Seafix headphones. It was time for drastic measures. Something had to be done to increase the apparent wind.

That was how I came to turn round and sail back in the direction of Falmouth for three hours.

And it wasn't only peaked caps and Mrs Thatcher who held us up. Look what happened at the start: first of all, Radio Cornwall informed the country that we were off on a twelve *thousand* mile race and then the Met Office's south-westerly Force six, occasionally gale 8, left me in a state of such apprehension that I spent more time trying to stay as far away as possible from all the other competitors than I did trying to get near the starting line.

And then the new headsail furling gear turned itself back to front. Now, I'm not going to mention which make it is because I'm sure that somehow it's my fault that I've had nothing but trouble with it ever since I got it.

But the fact is that it didn't work when it was brand new, it stopped working a week before the start, and three days into the race, the fitting at the top turned round and jammed the spinnaker halyard.

This could have been solved almost at once by a quick trip up the mast – but, as I said to myself, I'd have to take the sail off, and that would slow us down, which wouldn't do at all.

It's not as if I mind going up the mast – not at all. I'd spent most of the week in Falmouth up there, and I'm sure some of the tourists thought I must be some sort of fixture.

But, given the choice, with the boat rolling through 20° - and particularly with no one around to call me chicken, I decided I'd rather keep my feet on the deck. Besides, with twin headsails, we were still doing nearly five knots.

Excuses like that, of course, are only good until the wind dies. By the time the log line was hanging straight up and down, I was reduced to huffing round the boat, saying things like: "If Naomi James can climb the mast in the Southern Ocean…"

Of course, Naomi James had steps up the mast. I didn't. Worse still, I had a block and tackle that wasn't quite long enough to reach the deck. It had worked well enough in Falmouth, where I developed a system using one hand to hold the block upright and the other for clipping the bo'sun's chair to it. Observant readers will notice this does not leave a hand for holding on – which, on a mooring off the Royal Cornwall Yacht Club, did not seem to matter too much. In a 4ft Atlantic swell, it suddenly became a matter of the most pressing importance.

By the time I had slid down the mast and impaled a delicate part of my anatomy on the key for the spinnaker ring, comparisons with Naomi James began to give way to reminders that I was supposed to be doing this for fun and that the medical kit lacked anything in the way of serious painkillers.

So, Dr Maginnes gets the blame for *Largo* spending five days of tailwinds without a spinnaker.

He had been adamant. I had gone to see him armed with a list of suggested drugs. Some of them sounded really exciting and came in ampules, but all Dr Maginnes wrote was a prescription for boring old antibiotics.

"You can get Paracetamol over the counter," he said, scribbling.

"But that's not going to be enough. What if I break a wrist or something?"

"Then you take your Paracetamol and remind yourself you're British."

Oh great: A doctor from the Boys' Own School of Medicine. "By Gad, Carruthers, I've lost me leg!"

"No, you haven't, sir. It's over here."

I could see it all: 700 miles from the nearest hospital, it wouldn't seem so funny.

Of course, John Elliott on *Shoki* the first 30, managed the situation much better. Not only did he retrieve his spinnaker halyard by going up the mast on his Jumar mountaineering gear but, having led it the wrong way through the masthead diamond, he managed to resolve the situation without going up again.

He described his solution one night in Ponta Delgada as if it was an exercise he might set the students of his Scottish sailing school: "I reckoned that if I attached a weight to the halyard, I could hoist it up, wait until it swung the right side of the wire and then let it down. The problem lay in finding something heavy enough but at the same time something that wouldn't demolish the mast or go smashing through the sails."

A turnip turned out to be ideal. Sailing instructors based on the Clyde carry turnips as essential equipment, apparently - thus lending a completely new slant to H.L. Tilman's advice never to set foot on a boat without an onion.

Still, even if I never did get up the mast, the five days were still quite something. After we had logged 137 miles in 24 hours, I took to standing in the companionway making "Ee-har" noises like a Western stagecoach driver as we charged down the Atlantic rollers with Arnold the Aries working overtime and the wake stretching brilliant white, seemingly all the way to the horizon.

By this stage, of course, I'd stopped worrying about the race and was feeling mightily contented. I even wrote an account of the daily round in the logbook as if it was some sort of guide to The Meaning of Life.

It goes like this: *A couple of extra 40-minute kips after I should really have got up – I decided 40 minutes is not too long in this superb visibility. Then breakfast is either muesli or a boiled egg, then lovely fresh bread and fresh coffee.*

Then there's the morning sight (trying to get the azimuth as near as possible to 90° for longitude).

Hot chocolate and digestives at mid-morning, then feed the animals - that's a drop of oil for the Aries and maybe, the log.

The noon sight usually comes before lunch since I try to arrange meals late so that dinner arrives close to midnight, thereby cutting down the time I'm asleep in darkness. Lunch is packet soup and sandwiches and then tea with bread and jam. If I make the bread in the afternoon, I get it still warm from the oven.

Finally, I award myself a whisky before dinner and then bed around 0100 or 0200 with the alarm clock in the corner of the bunk set for 40 minutes.

One way and another, I do have a lot of spare time since I'm not steering when the wind is steady as it is today. There's little to do but read a bit, occasionally work out where we are and how far there is to go and then spend the rest of the time sitting in the sun watching over the boat. It's not unpleasant and has the added advantage that I can spot things which are not as they should be before something nasty happens.

By the time I started getting near The Azores, I'd reached the rather unnecessary state of mind where I wanted to make the landfall using just the sextant and without checking the RDF beacons – silly really. When the light on Ponta de Arnel showed up just after dusk, I was five miles further east than I need have been.

But there's nothing like the presence of other boats to revive the competitive spirit. *Aphrodite,* the Moody 39, was just ahead. I could hear them on the VHF, constantly revising their ETA as they sat becalmed off the south coast. But then, *Aphrodite's* crew were rather unusual in racing circles – a pair of surgeons from the Hamble, they had a pet geranium and, after the first week, they changed into dinner jackets and opened champagne for the Captain's cocktail party. I crept up on them in the night.

I was woken by the Watchman beeping a warning. I looked round: flat calm but no ship. The microchips do that sometimes. Five minutes later, they were beeping with a regularity that brooked no argument. I got the binoculars out and there, straight out of the rising sun, came a freighter with masts in line and a bow wave that could swamp a lifeboat. I began to feel concerned. The batteries were flat again – I couldn't even motor out of the way.

When she was about 400 yards away and still coming straight for me, I decided it was time to feel frightened. I jumped below and called him up on VHF, hoping the last gasp of the batteries would be enough to transmit at least a watt. No response. I grabbed the foghorn and a lifejacket as well. As I passed the chart table on the way back, *Aphrodite* called up, all chatty with morning freshness.

"Can't talk now," I said, snatching up the microphone. "There's a ship 400 yards away heading straight for me."

My voice, as Stan Simmons, *Aphrodite's* skipper described it later, was "heavy with tension". For good measure, I added: "If you don't hear from me again. Would you raise the alarm, please."

He came back: "What is your position?"

Oh hell, I had no time to work out a position. I spread a couple of fingers across the chart: "About five miles south of Ponta Arnel." In fact, it was three, but he could see me when he knew where to look.

The ship came on. I tooted the horn – which had never sounded so puny. I thought about a smoke flare but realised it wouldn't make any difference: if a lookout couldn't see me as I was, floodlit by the morning sun, with all sail up and broadside on, then he certainly wouldn't see a smoke flare.

I started to work out what would happen: a glancing blow would throw *Largo* to one side. Would she float long enough for me to launch the dinghy, or should I start blowing it up now?

And then I saw a glint of sun on the ship's side. Imperceptibly, she was turning.

The ship passed about 50 yards away. A man came out onto the wing of the bridge and waved. He just wanted to come and have a look at me. I sat in the cockpit with my hands over my head.

It was some time before I remembered to call *Aphrodite* and tell them I was all right. Stan said he'd watched the whole thing. He said it looked very nasty. I told him: "You should have seen it from here."

That story was told over and over again at the many parties in

Aphrodite's gigantic cockpit. The only event that prompted more interest was Stanley's sister-in-law sitting on the geranium.

But I had my own excitements. I phoned home and discovered I'd made the back page of the *Daily Telegraph*. It was rather like Captain Hornblower reading an account of his own heroics in *The Gazette*. Suddenly I was a famous ocean-racing yachtsman – and I hadn't even been trying. What would they say if I put down Frederick Forsyth and pulled up a spinnaker?

I resolved to try harder on the way back. I gave myself the target of getting home in time for my elder son's end-of-term. Fourteen days didn't seem too difficult. The trip out had only taken thirteen-and-a-half.

I might have managed it, too – if I'd got up in time for the start. As it was, I was still buying eggs when other people were rigging spinnaker sheets. I ended up watching them march away from me in a blaze of multi-coloured nylon and the following morning found me becalmed, still within 10 miles of the start line and totally alone. What made it worse was that I could hear boats only just over the horizon complaining they only had a southerly Force 2 while the leaders were churning along at five knots.

Not that I complained, you understand. Complaining about calms does no good at all. The management of calms is a very delicate business, and on the way back, I had plenty of opportunity to study the subject.

Essentially, there are two ways of dealing with calms. The first assumes there is somebody in charge of the weather, in which case it's as well to show pathetic gratitude for the situation, tug at the forelock, grovel a bit and mutter apologetically: "It's too good for me, Sir. Oh, I don't deserve it, Sir." I find a stage West Country accent works quite well. Self-flagellation with the end of a jib sheet can be added in more serious cases.

Alternatively, there is the varnish technique. This works on the well-known principle that there is nothing, absolutely nothing, more likely to produce a rain squall than wet varnish.

By the end of the first week, *Largo's* varnish gleamed like something out of Earls Court, and I was a snivelling wreck – and we still weren't going to get back in time for the end of term.

I became utterly preoccupied with the weather, plotting maps I didn't understand from the shipping forecast, begging every merchantman I met for a forecast.

I stopped this nonsense after the radio operator on a Russian grain ship informed me that I could expect a south-westerly Force 10. He meant 10 metres per second, and he'd been looking at arrows on a weather map. They were pointing *to* the southwest.

Still, it was wind, and while it blew, we beat into it. When it stopped, we sat still for a day or two and got dragged inexorably into the Bay of Biscay. I began to play *I spy with my little eye*. It lacked something.

In the end, it took me 17½ days to reach Falmouth. There was one gallon of diesel left and no digestive biscuits. I was reduced to reading the adverts in *Reed's* – starting at the beginning. I was the second to last boat in. I'd have to rush back to work, and the *Daily Telegraph* ignored me.

But I had sailed 2,400 miles without breaking anything important, and I'd ended up where I was supposed to.

And I still had my hat.

Chapter 5
The Three-Year Itch

The water was over the cabin sole – or, at least, it would have been if the cabin sole had not been floating three inches above its rightful place.

It was time to get a new boat.

Odd, isn't it, what happens to the boat you bought so enthusiastically just a few years ago – which you boasted about in the bar (a real bargain, beautiful nick and goes like the clappers). Suddenly she's damp and sluggish, and the best you can find to say about her is that she might fetch enough to pay for one of those new, lightweight cruiser-racers.

The RYA hasn't yet commissioned a survey into the three-year-itch, but that's what it is – as predictable as a gale in August and just as troublesome. No matter what plans you think you may have; after the third season, everything changes.

The substantial blue water cruiser - the "proper boat" that was going to open up new horizons -suddenly becomes an old tub that won't shift without half a gale behind her.

Or the home-completed bargain that you bought instead of the small but yard-built alternative: notice how you begin to lose patience with the lockers that never completely close or the table that collapses in the middle of dinner, or inevitably, the sink that leaks directly into the cutlery drawer.

The three-year itch means that boats which were bought as day-sailers with a cuddy for boiling a kettle are suddenly condemned as wholly unsuitable for a fortnight's cruise, while cruising boats, in turn, end up on the market because they're hugely expensive to keep and really need a paid hand to stay on top of the varnish.

The third season; that's when it strikes. Over two whole summers, I had grown used to sliding back the hatch and being greeted by the unmistakable fetid smell of mildew and sodden sleeping bags, but I couldn't take it for a third year. As I set to pumping. I remember wondering how long it would have taken for the boat to sink.

I used to spend a lot of time pumping in that little boat. The man who built her made a small mistake in marking the position for the keel bolts. The holes ended up a sort of elliptical shape, and over the years, they were packed with just about type of sealant from good old caulking cotton to the very latest heavily-advertised all-purpose gunge.

None of these ever did the slightest good, of course - just as they never did any good in stopping the water from getting under the fibreglass sheathing in the cockpit. When I sold her, I had the keels dropped off one more time for the buyer - just to show willing.

I often wonder, as I pump out the pint from the stern gland of the Rival 32 I bought in her place, just how many times she's had them off since.

I have to keep wondering because, if I didn't, I'd become sentimental every time I saw a Caprice bobbing on its tidal mooring – because it's true that just as disenchantment sets in after three years, nostalgia arrives after six.

Readers who have a talent for arithmetic will have realised by now that nostalgia for the first boat arrives to coincide conveniently with disenchantment over the second.

This can cause a certain confusion and might explain why I found myself driving 200 miles to look at a boat 6ft shorter than the one I've got. All I could think about was what I have to pay for a mooring, the horrendous estimate I'd had for a new genny and why they won't let me into Lyme Regis anymore.

Somehow the 6ft I'd be losing seemed less important than banks of wind instruments and sails that hadn't acquired the shape of carrier bags.

I actually stood in the cabin and asked myself what did it matter if the only headroom was under the hatch.

I went for a trial sail, slipping along nicely with the merest breath of wind – conditions which would have left the Rival drifting around in circles. But what I should have been wondering was how a 26footer would have behaved in last year's gale off Ushant. Would I have been quite so nonchalant about putting a stew in the pressure cooker with a lightweight hull leaping right out of the water?

But then, we all forget, don't we? Who actually makes a point of remembering the unfortunate incident of the mulligatawny soup?

It happened rather by accident after missing the tide round St Catherine's Point in the Caprice. For four-and-a-half hours, I bucketed up and down in the same spot, and in the middle of it all, the soup leapt off the stove, upended itself on the floor and, by the time I'd slithered around trying to mop it up, I looked like some sort of highly-spiced mud-wrestler.

My father's just the same. From the comfort of his 36ft Halbardier – steadfastly maintained to Lloyds 100A1 – he mellows and talks affectionately of his first boat, also an 18footer (albeit with a six-foot bowsprit). His leaked not only from the bottom upwards but also from the deck downwards. "The forepeak was a very nasty place," he says with fond memory. "If you couldn't dry your sails, they used to rot."

The 18footer came with a 10ft dinghy which he towed all over the South Coast. On windy trips back over Chichester Bar, it would try to climb into the cockpit. He kept it at bay with the deck brush.

"Ah, they don't make them like that anymore," says Father, adjusting the autopilot a touch and dropping another ice cube into his gin.

I grew up thinking I was missing something because we never blew out a sail, and my bunk was always dry.

Of course, we did have our moments – with a family of five in a Folkboat, that was inevitable. Folkboats don't have five berths, and so someone had to sleep on a Li-Lo on the floor. Father approved of this. It showed we could rough it. But he became terribly forgetful when rising to check the warps as he liked to do sometime around 0300. The sequence of events never varied; very gently, so as not to wake anyone, he would step out of his bunk and onto my sister's face.

No matter how gently he did this, she never failed to scream. Nor did the rest of us fail to sit bolt upright and crash our skulls on the deckhead. Then we would scream too.

Twenty-five years on, all that we choose to remember is that five of us really did get to Holland in that little boat – just as I now recall not the mulligatawny off St Catherin's Point but sailing back into Poole afterwards, breakfasting on boiled eggs and throwing the shells over my shoulder. The boats coming out of the harbour assumed I'd sailed overnight from France – which did my self-esteem no harm at all.

If incidents like that can emerge transformed by the act of memory, imagine what happens to the good times.

Good times like the first real Channel crossing when we set the Autohelm off the Needles and didn't touch it again until we met the ferry coming out of Cherbourg.

Or the day in the marina at Lésardrieux, when a Frenchman stepped off something at least twice as big, paused beside us and mused: "Ah, so small but so beautiful."

And the crew, bikini-clad in the cockpit, fluttered and preened.

After a while, the old photographs come out and, somehow you forget that, with three people in the cockpit, the self-drainers used to drain inwards or that the sheet winches were on back to front and the radar reflector obscured the burgee – or even that the cables inside the mast slapped horribly in anything more than a ripple.

To hear some of us go on, you'd think there would be a brisk trade in second-hand boats. You'd think the brokers would be run off their feet instead of sitting over Calor heaters drinking instant coffee all day. You'd imagine magazines would be filled with adverts and boatyards crawling with owners furtively trying to clinch a deal without handing over 1% to the yard.

Well, that might have been the case if only the Almighty, when He set Noah up in the boatbuilding business, hadn't also invented winter.

The relevant passage in Genesis doesn't usually get much publicity because clergymen, having to work on Sundays, tend not to go in for yachting. But it is a fact that, when the flood subsided, Noah laid up the Ark and stood there surrounded by sleeping bags and coils of running rigging and suddenly came over all sentimental.

For there is nothing - absolutely nothing - quite so pathetic as the sight of a yacht out of the water. Even polished up to look good for the queue of buyers and even supposing you did manage to get a couple of coats of varnish on her at the beginning of September, she's still as forlorn as the last toy on the shelf.

So, all her little faults get forgiven for another year, or at the very least, they get written down on a list of things that never get done.

And another year will see that locker falling open again, and more apologies for the table and the rusty spoons until eventually something happens – some unforgettable disaster strikes, some ultimate family row develops – and suddenly there's no going back.

For some people impending divorce works quite well. Others opt for a more dramatic solution – like being presented with the wooden spoon at the laying up dinner for coming last overall.

But personally, I find there's nothing, absolutely nothing, quite so effective as a foot of water in the cabin.

Chapter 6
The OSTAR

In 1988, I fulfilled my great ambition and sailed Largo in the Singlehanded Transatlantic Race. The Evening Standard gave me time off (indeed it had been a pre-requisite of accepting the job). In order to justify this, they gave me a single-sideband radio to send back despatches as I went along. In those days, this was done by dictating to a "copy-taker" sitting at a typewriter with a pair of headphones clamped over his ears.

These copytakers are now extinct, but they were as idiosyncratic as the dinosaurs – and just as cantankerous. This meant that if you dictated at the height of a gale off the Grand Banks and happened to mention that the decks were "spume-filled", they would just as likely type "fume-filled". The sub-editors had no idea what was going on and just pushed it through.

I have left the howlers as they were printed – for authenticity.

TUESDAY 31st MAY.

The greatest moment of my life will arrive at 12 noon on Sunday 5th June. I'm very lucky. Not everyone has such a prompt appointment with ecstasy. That is when I will sail my boat over the starting line of the greatest single-handed race in the world and set course for America.

Me and 100 others - each with our own reasons for wanting to sail alone across the notoriously violent Atlantic, where the only certainty is that we shall be wet and cold and uncomfortable. We will be permanently tired, often frightened and probably lonely as well. The last time someone came up to me and said, "Why?" I told them: "It's fun, you should try it sometime." Which is a bit like describing the 1812 Overture as a rather jolly tune.

For me, this is not so much a race as an emotional experience. I've been living with it since I was 11. That was 1960 when my parents took me to the Walton and Frinton Yacht Club to hear a lecture by one Francis Chichester, who had just won the first race. I can't remember much about it except that he showed a slide of half a dozen dolphins diving in formation out of a breaking wave and hoped the race would be organised on a regular basis. I hoped so too.

I didn't want them abandoning it before I had a chance. I took to reading the books in which successful competitors described how ghastly it was for much of the time, but how they wouldn't have missed it for the world, and I made my plans: what kind of boat, which route to take, the best way to ride out a storm, that kind of stuff. It's easy when it's just a dream.

The dream crept into reality so slowly that it was impossible to say exactly when it became a fact. All I know is that five years ago when I sold my little boat and set out to look for one I could stand up in, I was also looking for a boat that would cross an ocean. I found a Rival 32 called 'Margo', and my superstition against changing boats' names relented only to the extent of one letter: I re-christened her 'Largo'. She might have continued to potter about the Channel if it had not been for an unexpected fortnight when I found myself without a crew. Five days after leaving Poole, I arrived at Santander - feeling as if I would burst with satisfaction.

Excitement of that kind really ought to be shared. Going out for a solitary meal and hoping for a chatty waitress is not enough. That's why races like this one are ideal for normal, gregarious people who just happen to like sailing on their own. We're an assorted bunch because this race is like that. On the one hand, you have the gigantic lightweight catamarans and trimarans on huge sponsorship budgets, and then there are the amateurs like me - without a hope of winning - but who view the idea of getting to the other side as a victory in its own right.

MONDAY 6th JUNE.

The great moment escaped in the confusion. Somewhere in the frenetic melee at the start of the race yesterday, I sailed 'Largo' across the line and completely forgot to savour the beginning of an adventure. The full realisation that, after all the planning, the race was finally on, came later when the chaos resolved itself into one of those days so perfect you could splice it onto the end of a Hollywood weepie.

But first there came the horror movie - the heart-stopping sight of the big yachts bearing down like brightly painted battering rams.

The Good Stuff – Book One

The start is generally considered to be the most terrifying part of the race. With 100 boats jockeying for position, all you need is a hatful of wind to turn the regatta into a creditable reconstruction of the Battle of the Nile. To begin with, we just drifted about in circles but when the wind did arrive, it merely turned three hours of aimless frustration into a combined competitive spirit not altogether desirable. At least half the skippers threw caution to what winds there were and aimed for the plum spot on the line. And yes, I was one of them.

I have a vague recollection of not being able to see any water. On one side, there was a Norwegian who had cut the front nine inches off his boat to get into a smaller class and on the other, a Frenchman who carried a 56lb bag of onions and threatened to melt any troublesome icebergs by breathing on them. Ahead there was an American flying an enormous flag and behind me, inevitably, was 'UAP 1992', the 60 ft satellite garden centre. The fleet parted before it. 'Largo, of course, got left behind. This may have had something to do with her age, her comfortable design or even the fact that she was laden with enough duty-free stores for both the outward and return voyages, but mostly it was because, ten minutes after King Constantine fired the starting cannon, 'Largo's skipper stopped worrying about the other boats and determined instead to enjoy the growing warm wind and sparkling sea as the boat romped past the Eddystone lighthouse towards the distant horizon.

MONDAY 13th JUNE.

Feeling a little jaded and not much like getting down to work, I threw a party last night. Before the Race Committee reach for the rule book and the bit about no physical contact with other boats at sea, I should explain that this was quite the most extraordinary party I have ever given: None of the guests actually met. It all started on the 'sked', the regular chat on the radio, on Saturday morning when James Hatfield silenced us all by remarking that he had been awarded the MBE in the Queen's Birthday Honours.

James is a remarkable young man, and the news that he was celebrating his latest honour with a solitary bottle of champagne some 800 miles out in the Atlantic was clearly unacceptable, so when British Telecom's maritime radio station at Portishead broadcast the weather forecast later that morning, they also announced the award and that a celebration would be held at 1945 GMT. So the evening found me sitting by Largo's radio in a white silk dinner jacket, neat black tie and with a bottle of champagne cooling in a bucket of Atlantic Ocean at my feet.

First arrival was Robin Knox-Johnston. He apologised for his oldest jeans, but he was sailing 'Suhaili', the boat which took him round the world in 1968 but leaks a bit. He'd spent the day trying to fix the engine. James arrived, saying he'd had terrible trouble getting a cab. Other guests checked in. Later, I drank a silent toast to the guests who couldn't make it - the many in this race who do not carry a long-range radio. For most, it is a matter of finance. Others, of course, really do enter these races for the solitude. As a Frenchman said in Plymouth when I explained about the radio and the Evening Standard: "Then you are not alone."

No, I suppose not, but neither am I going round the bend. I really do have a white silk dinner jacket on this boat.

FRIDAY 17th JUNE.

It was when the beansprouts hit the deck that the facade of civilisation finally cracked. Beansprouts are notorious. If it were only a matter of vitamins, then the Sanatogen tablets would be adequate - but Sanatogen tablets tossed in French dressing don't really go with pate de canard aux champignons. So beansprouts it had to be, and now they are everywhere - and this being a boat and somewhat damp, they are going to grow. By the time we get to America, I'll have to eat my way out of the cabin.

The boat's lurching had caused the beansprouts' centre of gravity to shift by six feet, but this time, it was not because we were romping steadily through the waves to Newport; it was because we were becalmed and rolling like a pig on wet clover. As another mariner, whose poetic sensibilities were presumably not interrupted by an airborne larder, once observed; the ocean never sleeps. So even though there are no actual waves, the swell remains, rolling the boat onto her ear and then two seconds later, onto her other ear.

It's been like that for two days now. The northerly wind, which blew so steadily for a week to send us shooting out into the ocean at unheard of speeds, stayed just long enough to ensure M . Poupon got his record, and then it stopped completely. The red ensign hung like a rag at the stern, and the rolling began. It's best when this happens to pretend it hasn't, to carry on with the jaunty air of one who knows his right and whose right includes a respectable breeze, and to mumble to oneself: "Ah, 'tis a fine wind, to be sure."

This does not, of course, make any difference, but it does stop an otherwise sentient being from degenerating into some lower form of life who stumbles about kicking the furniture. And usually, it works. It works very well, in fact, until the beansprouts take to the air. So, when what will certainly prove to have been not the last beansprout was finally retrieved from the bilges, a pathetic admonishing finger emerged from the hatchway and an hysterical voice announced: "Not a hand on a rope. You hear me? Not one finger on a rope until there is wind."

And with that the hatch slammed shut.

TUESDAY 21st JUNE.

Whatever it was that I was looking for in sailing the ocean alone, I believe I found it right here - 1200 miles from Land's End at 1.30 am.

It was after a dinner of chicken curry with a great handful of sultanas and a sunset that bled pink and violet across the sky. A sliver of moon was the finishing touch. This was the night to do what I had planned all along. I stood in the hatchway to watch the stars. I had a little book to show me which was which. One day I plan to take the sextant to them.

All this too, was perfect. I found Cassiopeia and Capella, Aldebaran and the Pleiades. And I looked about me at the long pale green carpet of phosphorescence that was the wake. It's a sight which never palls. Tiny organisms in the water light up as they're disturbed by the passing of the keel. Any movement in the water turns them on - the bow waves spreading out like green fire, waves in the distance flash like lighthouses on a distant shore.

And two torpedoes came out of the south and headed straight for the boat.

They came on at an astonishing speed, leaving long pencil-thin trails of light behind them. Just when it seemed they must hit and I found myself tensed for the explosion, the twin streaks turned and broke the surface with a soft "phot-phot".

The dolphins were back. They'd been around on and off all the way, playing about the boat but by night, covered in phosphorescence and to a lone sailor becoming very susceptible to changes in mood, they were unbearably wonderful. There were five of them. They switched and crisscrossed just a few feet below me, their hard supple bodies lit up like incandescent bullets as they passed effortlessly through the water, breathing with that characteristic exhalation.

I was up in the bows for nearly an hour. The wind increased, sending flurries of spray over my legs, but I couldn't be the first to go. When they finally left, I was stiff and cold. I limped back along the sidedeck and stood for a moment holding onto the rigging and looking out into the night. I called out to them. I called, "Goodbye."

Foolish, perhaps, but when I sat down, I found I had to wash my glasses. You have to do that when you get salt on them. Salt on the outside means spray, but salt on the inside - that's emotion.

THURSDAY 23rd JUNE.

It wasn't so very long ago that people in this position suffered from a nasty creeping feeling that at any moment, they were going to fall off the edge of the world. I can see their point. For the last fortnight, I've been watching the little crosses on the chart pick their way westwards, progressing in a somewhat haphazard fashion towards - not America but the Edge of the Chart.

The Hydrographer of the Navy presumably drew the North Atlantic four and a half feet wide on the assumption that anyone interested in what was on the other side would be getting there in something big enough to spread it out. But I've been looking at the same bit of chart long enough now to believe that the edge represents the edge of the known world and that when I turned it over, I'd find vague outlines of half-discovered continents and legends in copperplate script saying "Here be monsters". Also, I had the uncomfortable feeling that the ocean itself would somehow be represented differently - full of icebergs and covered in fog, for example, which is the traditional recipe for the second half of the race. So this morning, with more trepidation than ceremony, I turned the chart.

The most startling discovery was that it was clean. The eastern half had a coffee stain the size of Spain, situated just west of Ireland. Spain itself was obliterated with little calculations and the message: "Our galaxy will ultimately collide with the galaxy Andromeda which will cause a disturbance." (This is something I heard on the World Service and intend to use someday when I need an understatement).

Even the position fixes had about them an air of uncertainty. Instead of the precise crosses which the Hydrographer had intended, there was a series of dots and asterisks with lines and arrows running between them as if a spider with muddy feet was emigrating. So, if the chart is to be believed, we are now closer to the finish than the start. It's all downhill from here; at least it is if you don't inspect the keel too closely and make out the Labrador current, which brings down the icebergs, and the Gulf Stream that tries to push you back to Plymouth.

Then there are the Newfoundland Grand Banks with their fog and looming trawlers and the notes about "hydrocarbon exploration areas (see caution)". There's even a Funk Island, which shouldn't surprise anyone. Come to think of it, the Hydrographer might just as well have written "Here be monsters after all.

THURSDAY 30th JUNE.

With only 600 miles to go, it may be a little late, but I have at last started racing in earnest. Sitting here in the mess of dripping oilskins, towels that will never dry and an incongruous and discarded pair of carpet skippers, the discomfort is suddenly immaterial. The fact is that there is a gale shrieking out of the south and 'Largo' is romping towards the finishing line like a thoroughbred suddenly given her head.

Purely because I did get up at three this morning, struggle into clammy foul-weather clothes and slithered about the fume-filled deck setting the absolute maximum amount of sail, we are now shooting straight up the sides of the huge Atlantic rollers to break through the crests in a welter of spray and then go crashing into the trough beyond with a thud that shakes the boat from masthead to keel.

This is what they call "driving a boat" and is the reason for so many of the entries in this race retiring before they get this far. It is the sort of thing cruising yachtsmen frown on as sheer folly and bad seamanship to boot. But I spent a month rebuilding and strengthening this boat for just this moment, and now when she hurls her seven tons from the top of a 20 ft wall of water, it is with a solid, satisfying sensation rather like a pantechnicon crushing motorway cones.

Every time the motion eases, every time I look out of the window and find the sidedecks no longer running with water, I dive once more into those soggy oilies and cram on more sail like some demented clipper captain trying for the record. It hardly seems possible that this is the same pathetic figure who effectively withdrew from the race - not to mention the world at large - just because he was becalmed for two days. Where did this glory-hungry ocean tiger come from?

The end is somehow tangible now. In fact, with the depth recorder, I can touch 60 metres beneath the keel. It might not be what you call shallow water in the normal course of things, but it is a singular improvement on figures like 4500 metres which we've had for the previous three weeks.

MONDAY 4th JULY.

As an hallucination, the stranger in the forecabin was hardly convincing, but in a race which is turning out to be not nearly as lonely as its name suggests we're rather short on the paranormal.

All the same, it can give you a nasty turn, after a month alone, to be confronted by an oilskin-clad figure standing swaying gently with the motion of the boat. It doesn't last long, of course, just long enough to realise that this is your own suit of oilskins hanging up to dry.

Personally, I found it a tremendous disappointment. I've been looking forward to a really impressive hallucination ever since I took up single-handed sailing. The combination of mild exhaustion and solitude provides a fragile environment for the wilder side of the imagination, and at some stage in a voyage, I can usually expect to sense a creeping certainty that I am not alone. But this trip is different because I have the long-range radio. Officially it's for sending back these despatches, but I use it shamelessly not so much to bolster my sanity with a little human contact as to lead a social life so busy that I have to keep a diary of appointments and stick notes above the chart table. There's the family to call and friends who have left messages of goodwill, but I do most of my talking with the people who share this experience - the other competitors.

When things were grim, when the boat was being tossed about by a gale and I was tumbled around a cabin in which everything not tied down had hurled itself into a puddle on the floor, then it was comforting to hear that life on the other boats was just as awful. Eventually, the sense of humour would surface, and someone would say: "Don't you have a maid to clean that up?"

Also, it was cheering to know that if things should go wrong, help was within a hundred miles or so. In fact, when I was thrown across the cockpit and narrowly missed smashing in my front teeth on a winch, I need not have worried. Forty-five miles away was a surgeon who specialised in rebuilding faces - not only did he have a full operating kit on board, but also, said he would be prepared to make a house call.

It's a camaraderie unknown in other sports. You could almost say that we sail single-handed for the company.

MONDAY 11th JULY.

With 3,000 miles stretching out in the wake, it was the last four which became the most important. Like all the big moments in life, reaching the other side of the Atlantic came almost without warning.

After snatches of sleep which added up to only four hours in the last 48, with a lighthouse flashing with the precision of a dying light bulb and remembering that in the last race, one boat was wrecked just five miles from the finishing line, I might have missed it altogether.

For the first time in a fortnight, we were charging along with the rigging humming and the bow wave setting up an impossibly loud roar. I'd stopped thinking of my boat as a construction of rope, wire, Terylene and glass fibre. 'Largo' had come alive a long time ago, and now she was up and running to the finish and trusting me to point her in the right direction.

I couldn't believe that on the last night, I was going to turn out to be the weak link - but the fact was I didn't know where we were. I had known. I had navigated us down the coast of Nova Scotia, across the Nantucket Shoals, and brought us to within ten miles of Newport, Rhode Island and the finishing line - and, let's not be shy about this, success.

Now I'd lost us. The Brenton Reef Light Tower, the powerful beacon which has welcomed generations of single-handed sailors at the end of this race, was nowhere to be seen. In its place was a dim yellow light flashing in an entirely different and erratic sequence. I was aware of being overtired, knowing full well the kind of stupid mistakes I was likely to make in this condition. I began shaking my head over the chart, muttering unfinished sentences - all of them including the word 'impossible'. And, all the while, the feeble light flashed. It was quite some time before I thought to call the Coastguard. Sure, he would step out of his office and look.

Sure, a few minutes later, he confirmed that the light was out of 'synch' and yes, it was operating on reduced intensity. He announced the news with all the polite interest of one who views lighthouses as historical monuments. It's nice to see them still working in this day of computerised position finding. Evidently, it had did not occur to him that there are some of us who still need them just as much as the Clipper captains of old.

Maybe they too, once they had established that they really were where they ought to be, relaxed and stood swaying easily with the motion as the ship headed like an arrow for the harbour mouth. They did not worry unduly about a photographer colleague who might be unhappy about recording the event in almost total darkness - and nor, I confess, did I. I had earned this moment and nobody was going to make me wait a second longer for it.

So, as dawn came up on Friday, entry number 91 crossed the line exactly 32 days, 21 hours, 40 minutes and 30 seconds after leaving Plymouth.

Even if it was 22 days and 12 hours behind the winner, you'd never have guessed, not by the smile all over the skipper's face.

Chapter 7
Largo's OSTAR

– then I had to write it all over again for Yachting Monthly. It appears that this happened quite a lot – this re-telling of the same story again and again. I wondered whether I should engage in some judicious editing now that it is all being put together into one book (well, two, if you're going to be pedantic). But I like to think that each time I told a story, I gave it a new twist – and anyway, it is an old man's prerogative to go on and on...

The canapés were wedged in the sink. A bottle of champagne stood cooling in a bucket of Atlantic by the chart table, and I comforted myself that no one was likely to notice I wasn't wearing cufflinks.

There are, after all, some advantages to giving a party 800 miles out in the Carlsberg Singlehanded Transatlantic Race.

The invitations had gone out after Portishead Radio's 1100 weather bulletin. In tones that might have done equally well for a vigorous low moving quickly east, the operator explained: "Competitors might like to know that James Hatfield of *Largo* has been awarded the MBE in the Birthday Honours. Anyone who would like to congratulate him will find him on 4143.5MHz at 1900 GMT."

Like the weather, this was true in parts. James *had* been awarded the MBE for raising money for charity while sailing alone around the world. He would most certainly be coming up on the single sideband schedule when a bunch of us met up on 4243.5MHz three times a day. It was just that his boat was called *British Heart III*. I was sailing *Largo*.

And that was how I came to host the oddest, most memorable and certainly the most enjoyable party I have ever given – even if none of the guests actually met.

We were, at this stage, spread out over hundreds of square miles of ocean. But, after a week alone at sea, during which the only human contact had been over the radio, the idea of us being separated by distance seemed somehow to have got lost along the way.

So there seemed nothing odd, at 1900, sitting by the set, tweaking at the cuffs of a ridiculous white silk dinner jacket and trying to stop the champagne sliding all over the floor.

Robin Knox-Johnston was the first to arrive, his voice coming over crisp and clear from somewhere 300 miles to the south. He brought a bottle of Cutty Sark but had been tinkering with Suhaili's engine all day and hadn't had time to change. I told him to go through to the drawing-room where people wearing frilly aprons were handing round canapés.

James Hatfield, the guest of honour, was next – and full of apologies. He said he'd had terrible trouble getting a cab. Others arrived. Are Wiig, being Norwegian, thought the MBE was some sort of prize. I attempted to transmit the sound of a champagne cork popping and dropped the microphone. It bounced tantalisingly on the edge of the bucket before I grabbed it and spilled a mixture of champagne and seawater all over my feet. James ran off with one of the people in frilly aprons.

It was only afterwards that it dawned on me that we had proved that singlehanded races are not nearly as lonely as everyone seems to imagine.

Start painting numbers on the deck and hang an Aries off the back, and, immediately, a small crowd gathers on the pontoon asking: "Why do you do it?" and "Don't you get lonely?" People on neighbouring boats tell each other quietly: "He always was a loner."

Listen to the rest of the world and you'd imagine we couldn't wait to get away from the whole lot of them and that the social side of life in Plymouth consists of ninety-six people standing on their own in the Carlsberg tent, staring into their beer and wondering how soon they can decently slip away.

But in fact, the embarrassingly-named Atlantic Challenger Bar was heaving every evening. Parties started on boats for no better reason than someone came asking to borrow a hacksaw, and there happened to be a beer open. The restaurants of The Barbican set new records for accepting bookings for two and then having to push tables together to accommodate six.

For the plain fact is that solo sailors are not a breed apart. There is not something different in their characters which makes them incapable of relating to the rest of the world. Those sorts of people slip quietly from their moorings on a Friday night without a word to a soul and are next heard of in Panama. In fact, most of the sailors in races like the Carlsberg and the Azores and Back do it for the company.

I didn't realise any of this at the time, of course. It never occurred to me that our little party was the highlight of the evening for plenty of others who couldn't be there because they only had SSB receivers. It wasn't until we got to Newport and discovered that all sorts of unlikely people were acquainted with our sense of humour that we began to realise just how important the radio schedule had been for everyone.

Peter Keig in *Zeal* called it: "Hatfield's Half Hour" – and certainly the dialogue did owe something to vintage radio comedy:

British Heart: "Morning *Largo*, how are you?"

Largo: "Terrible. The boat's in a frightful mess. What with Nigel throwing Charlotte Russe all over the ballroom and the band getting drunk and pushing the grand piano in the swimming pool... by the way, the caterers say they're missing a person in a frilly apron, you haven't got one have you?"

British Heart: "Yes, she's here – although she hasn't got her apron anymore. By the way, can I have my lawnmower back?"

Largo: "That went in the swimming pool too."

British Heart: "Damn. The polo ponies don't like it if the grass gets too long. How's Nigel? *Piper Rising*, this is *British Heart*..."

Piper Rising: "Hi James, I'm fine but I got stopped by the police for driving through a high-pressure zone without due care and attention. Sorry to hear *Largo's* in a mess. Shall I send the maid over to clean up?"

Eventually, of course, we returned to discussing our progress, but even that consisted of such rubbish as:

British Heart: "*Soren Sophie*, where are you this morning?"

Soren Sophie: "Hello James, I have now reached 48°W. I am at 48°01'W 31°12'N. Where are you today?"

British Heart: "I'm where you were yesterday and a bloody mess you left the place in too."

Of course, not everyone appreciated this sort of thing. The

magnificent Frenchman François Borgeois made this clear in Plymouth when I told him I had an SSB. "With such a radio," he growled, "you are not truly alone. You will not find such a radio on my boat."

I looked at his boat, a beautiful 36footer called *Safar*. I classed her in the "dependable seaboat" category. However, he was quite right, she had no aerials.

But surely the rules demanded a VHF? François nodded gravely. "Handheld," he said, holding up a hand. "One watt and two channels. I have a range of one mile, but I do not use it."

I felt it best not to tell him about my experience on the AZAB when I had only VHF and how I switched on every evening and begged: "Is anyone there?"

After the Solent at a weekend, the idea of not finding anyone listening within a 20-mile radius takes some getting used to. But it is remarkable how quickly you do end up on your own. On that race, I talked to a fellow competitor off Ushant and then not again until I was in sight of the island of San Miguel ten days later.

So, one tends to rely on passing shipping for conversation. That is probably because a 250,000-ton bulk carrier is easier to see on the horizon than another 32ft yacht – and it's only when you see someone that you think to call them.

Although, of course, in the beginning, I didn't presume to do anything of the kind. It only started after I had left the VHF switched on after my plaintive "Is there anyone there?" session of the night before. So I was rather startled to hear someone whistle at me from the cabin.

The first thought, of course, was that this was the hallucination I had been expecting. All solo sailors worth their salt hope to experience their own version of Slocum's Pilot of the Pinta appearing at the helm.

The only trouble was that I had not been battling a gale for three days without a rest. I had not eaten goat's cheese and plums, and I doubted that even peanut butter and honey sandwiches would produce the same effect.

It took me a ridiculously long time to realise there was no point in looking in the boat for the phantom whistler and once I thought to scan the horizon, there – passing at a companionable three miles – was a rusty freighter.

Not knowing quite how to call up a total stranger, I plucked the microphone from its bracket and whistled back.

This time I got a voice: "Hello, sailing boat..." He turned out to be a Greek-registered motor vessel in ballast from Leningrad to Charleston to pick up grain. We had a long chat. He was so impressed to hear about the race and the fact that I was alone, he even went to get his captain and I had to explain it all over again. It quite made my day.

Of course, merchant seamen tend to get rather bored and are only too happy to chat. The trouble is that, for the yachtsman, after the first half-dozen times, the novelty begins to wear thin. Even the most troublesome ego can get enough of the incredulous: "You mean you are alone? You have no crew? There is no one else aboard your ship?"

Much more fun was running into a Swede slap in the middle of the Atlantic. We only ran into each other metaphorically, of course; actually, we never saw each other at all. But he had a yacht in sight and was trying to make contact while I was over the horizon but with the VHF switched on.

I soon discovered why the Swede had been so anxious to talk. He was in a Vertue and had set out from Venezuela intending to stop in the Caribbean on his way home, but when he got to the right latitude he found he was enjoying himself so much, he decided to keep going.

So instead, he headed for The Azores but after a few days, that seemed a pointless detour too, and now he was plodding straight up the middle of the Atlantic with the vague idea of calling at the Faeroe Islands. Since he didn't have a chart of the area, and I thoroughly frightened him with an account I'd read somewhere of 10-knot tides between the islands, he decided not to go there either. Besides, he was getting to like the idea of doing Venezuela to Sweden non-stop.

We chatted for an hour until I got hungry, and then after dinner, he called again, saying he would like me to send a telegram to his mother after all. Personally, I think he just wanted to talk some more, so we covered the state of his clothes (going rather mouldy) and the beansprouts which I had somehow managed to spill all over the cabin, and were now growing in some very peculiar places indeed. We didn't say goodbye until the transmissions started breaking up.

It was odd, really, that we found so much to talk about. In my weekly calls home, I was becoming progressively tongue-tied. It seemed ridiculous to go on about the weather, although out there, the weather was the single most important part of life. Meanwhile, news of goings on ashore seemed to lack something in the way of reality.

Up until then, I had been setting two alarm clocks so that I woke up every 40 minutes for a look around. I know it's technically possible for a ship to appear over the horizon and run down a yacht in 30 minutes but for that, they have to be heading straight for each other and both going at full speed – and if I was going to be that unlucky, then the floating container would get me anyway.

So there I was crawling out of bed all the time and still only seeing ships at the rate of one every three or four days, when I discovered I was the only one daft enough to do this. As an experiment, I set the alarm, just once, for 90 minutes.

It was wonderful. It was like a lie-in on a Sunday morning, knowing that someone else is getting breakfast. I slept soundly for an hour. Then would you believe it, the Watchman radar detector went off.

This usually heralds a ship about three miles away. I grumbled, spent a minute getting myself up and putting on my shoes. Slowly, I hauled myself into the companionway.

And there, about 100ft away was the biggest trawler I had ever seen. I knew very well that small ship's radars failed to set off the Watchman until the last minute but what was a trawler doing here? He should be on the Grand Banks. I was prepared to stay awake practically round the clock when I got there.

But there he was, ablaze with lights, churning along at a steady five knots with his engine straining. Everything else on the ocean would get out of his way for the very good reason that with everything he had dragging behind him, his rudder wouldn't have any effect anyway.

I stood there and stared at him and felt sick and dizzy. There was no point in going about now he was past me, and anyway, there was less chance of fouling his cables if I kept the boat heeled. All I could think about was that we were steering by Aries and how the tiniest shift of wind would have put us under his bow instead of his stern.

Of course, I had no trouble staying awake after that. I paced from the chart table to the galley and then turned round and took the one pace it takes to get back again. Every ten paces, I leapt onto the step and scanned the horizon – nothing.

I realised, after a while, that this was ridiculous. I switched on the radio. I was just beginning to hear the Newfoundland MW station during the hours of darkness.

But, since this was three o'clock in the morning and even Newfoundlanders don't provide much of a radio audience at three in the morning, we had the minority interest show. At that moment, I would have been happy with a talk on goat breeding or English for new Canadians.

What I got was a man with a Georgia accent telling me: "You turned away from God!"

He pronounced it: "Gaad".

Who, me?

"Yes, you! You turned your back on Him!"

It was awful. There was this ghastly man, who probably had a white suit covered in rhinestones and a billion-dollar mission, and he had me exactly where he wanted me. And, since he put it like that. Yes, I did prefer to go sailing on Sundays.

But he wouldn't let go. And I, who knew with great certainty that I was only alive by the merest chance, was quite unable to switch him off. He harangued me for ten minutes before he got me down on my knees. I felt ridiculous. But more than that, I felt very frightened indeed.

In the morning, I just felt ridiculous. I certainly wasn't going to write about this. I'd have every religious nut in London after me.

In fact, it wasn't until I got my feet on solid ground again and the office demanded a final article, that I wrote about it. They wanted an analysis of my state of mind. The headline was already written. It said: "Did I go mad?"

So I sat there looking over a Massachusetts cornfield and opened up the little portable computer that had travelled all the way in the dry food locker, took a deep breath and decided that this, too, was part of the whole adventure.

Of course, I told them that I didn't go mad. I told them that I wanted to do it again and that the next time I heard the dolphins talking to me through the hull, I bound once more on deck, calling a welcome.

I made a reasoned case that the oceans were made to be sailed and the sun and the wind come free, and I suggested that all of this was a good deal more sane than much of what goes to make up the news bulletins I had left behind.

But that wasn't what convinced them. In the end, it was a rather shaky photograph taken 800 miles out with the camera clamped to the rail that did the trick.

You see, I really did wear that awful dinner jacket.

Chapter 8
Real Men Don't Use Spinnaker Squeezers

The spinnaker pole was cranked up like a gun barrel, pointing dead ahead and up at 45°. The sail itself flogged somewhere to leeward.

Eventually, it grabbed the wind and hauled *Largo* over and down, dunking the side deck as far as the coachroof and sending me sliding across the foredeck.

I held on, one leg in the water, an arm around the samson post and willed the self-steering to bring us out of the broach. The downhaul, easing itself on the over-full cleat, allowed the pole to scrape up the forestay another yard.

Then suddenly everything lit up with half a million candlepower as the spinnaker guy popped the lifebuoy out of its bracket and the strobe light went with it, righting as it says in the instructions and beginning to flash.

The reality of Force 6 to the west of the Grand Banks did not look any better when you could see it. The big seas were frozen in monochrome to leeward, the spinnaker hung in delicate curves as if floating on a windless afternoon – and everywhere there were drops of water, crystallised in the electronic moment.

And then Maurice Chevalier began to sing *Thank Heaven for Little Girls*.

At this point, I started to giggle.

There was not, of course, anything particularly funny about the situation: A lifetime ambition to sail the Singlehanded Transatlantic Race seemed in imminent danger of collapsing along with the mast. Any moment the boat would respond to the urgings of the autopilot and hurl herself into a gybe – and I was far too busy stopping myself sliding downhill into the Atlantic to have much impression on events.

In fact, the only semblance of normality was the unflappable Chevalier oozing from the cassette player in the cabin as if the only way to deal with the unexpected is to take one's hat and cane and go for a stroll in the *Bois de Bologne*.

But then, I had been behaving out of character ever since the wind picked up in the late afternoon, and I decided to start racing.

With only 600 miles to go to the finishing line in Newport, it was, admittedly, a little late to start – after all, Phillipe Poupon had got there a fortnight ago. By now, he was back in France, appearing on chat shows. But Fleury Michon was a 60ft tri. *Largo* was a Rival 32, and I always did spend too much time sitting and looking at sunsets.

So, when Poupon crossed the line, I was still a bit less than halfway, baking bread and talking to dolphins. It wasn't the winning that counted, I told the dolphins: it was the getting there.

But now that Newport was close enough to enter into the calculations, it seemed only reasonable to get there sooner rather than later. I set the spinnaker, put *Gigi* on the cassette player (she auto-reversed into South Pacific every 45 minutes) and settled down to do some serious steering.

I don't usually steer. It always seems such a terribly dull occupation – especially when one could be sitting in the sun reading a book or even perched in the companionway with a sundowner. But after a fellow competitor with a boat two feet shorter explained away a sudden lead of 30 miles by saying: "I was up all night driving my spinnaker", it seemed obvious that I ought to be doing the same.

If ever I had done such a thing before – which, let's face it, by this stage, I ought to have – I would have known about that subtle difference between controlling the spinnaker with that instant touch of the helmsman's hand on the tiller and allowing the beast to take over as you crawl forward with your heart in your mouth while the boat gets dragged from one side of the ocean to the other and the autopilot grinds away to itself while always remaining that awkward couple of seconds behind the situation.

In fact, there was a sort of tragic inevitability about the way I sat there filling myself with digestive biscuits and spewing out the crumbs to the tune of *Some Enchanted Evening* while *Largo* surged through the gathering dusk, her great spoon bow pushing out a rolling carpet of foam. When the breakers climbed up alongside, I delighted in the surge as we took off in a welter of spray, the log line spinning itself into a blur, before we were left wallowing for an instant until the spinnaker flipped itself open with a bang that thumped at the chainplates and *Largo* picked herself up out the water and charged forward once more. This was real sailing!

It all went splendidly until about midnight, when we got an awkward sea which wedged itself under the transom and hoiked the whole back end of the boat round to leeward. I leaned hard into the guardrails, the tiller under my chin as *Largo* broached luxuriantly.

In the cabin, Lesley Caron was inventing champagne while all around her, books, clothes, sodden towels and an itinerant Golden Delicious flung themselves from one side to the other – and then back again as I swooped across the cockpit pushing the tiller in front of me.

"An unlucky wave," I called down to Lesley, apologetically. "Nothing to worry about. Shouldn't happen again."

Of course it did. In fact, it began to happen with irritating regularity – and then a wave flopped itself right into the cockpit and something deep in the subconscious came to and announced: "Listen, it's blowing a good force six and rising. The sea is getting up, you're surfing out of control and pretty soon, something is going to break."

However, none of these problems seemed half as worrying as the prospect of getting the spinnaker down. Purely because I had always lowered it at the point where the autopilot started to lose control, I had never really found it much of a problem. I just unrolled the genny like a blanket, freed the guy, left the halyard once around the winch and took the tail forward to gather the 700sq ft of nylon underneath me rather as a mother duck sits on her eggs. There never really seemed to be the need for a spinnaker squeezer.

As I have been known to remark to impressionable ladies: "Real men don't use spinnaker squeezers".

Mind you, this was not something I mentioned out loud in Plymouth, not with my neighbour across the pontoon enlisting the help of his entire family to feed his kite into 40ft of nylon stocking – and particularly not when I recalled reading somewhere that he had been in the Royal Marines Special Boat Service, now ran an outward bound school and, for relaxation, competed in triathlons.

Also, I kept pretty quiet in the presence of another skipper who, having left things rather late on an Atlantic record attempt, brought up a parachute flare and reasoned that there was no quicker way of to take the sting out of a sail than by firing a handful of burning phosphorous into the middle of it – particularly if it was an old sail and had the last sponsor's logo all over it.

Of course, I should have taken warning from what happened when I arrived in Plymouth: I was in a dangerously contented frame of mind, savouring the prosect of mingling with all those famous yachtsmen milling around Queen Anne's Battery - the pontoons bristled with wing masts - television cameras for and aft. The sponsors had even laid on a small amount of beer – and *Largo* and I were going to be a part of all this. We sailed up to the breakwater with the spinnaker billowing like a peacock's breast.

Common sense took over when a ship appeared from the other end of the sound. Even famous singlehanders don't carry spinnakers up Plymouth Sound when there's a ship coming the other way. Leaving *Largo* in the care of the autopilot, I stepped forward smartly, intent on being sensible. I left the one turn on the winch and went forward with the tail of the halyard – the new halyard that I had reeved on the way down-Channel. I let out a little slack; nothing happened. I let out a little more. *Largo* ploughed on purposefully towards Plymouth.

I looked up to the top of the mast and there was the shiny new rope very obviously wrapped tightly round the fitting for the furling gear.

Taking hold of the sail, I gave a tug. What happened next was so inevitable that it was only astonishing that I should ever have bothered to register surprise. The spinnaker filled and lifted me effortlessly off the deck.

It was at this point that the party on the bridge of the ship sought to attract my attention by giving a blast on the horn. I waved one hand at the back of the boat – a gesture not covered in the semaphore section of *Brown's Manual of Signals* but which very obviously means: "I am manoeuvring with difficulty. You should pass astern of me."

Also, it had the effect of allowing the little bit of spinnaker I had managed to subdue to escape again so that *Largo* surged forward with renewed enthusiasm – straight for the eastern shore of the estuary.

It is on occasions like this, when disaster takes one by the lapels, that otherwise frail and fallible human beings are given the strength of those chaps in tights on children's television. I threw myself at the spinnaker. The spinnaker emptied itself in surprise, and the result was rather like strangling a souffle.

Together, we landed on the deck in a tangled blue heap. *Largo* stopped dead in her tracks, and the ship scraped by 50 yards astern with everyone out on the wing of the bridge. I swear I could hear sarcastic applause.

If it hadn't happened, then maybe I would have taken the episode that occurred on the Grand Banks almost exactly a month later a little more seriously. As it was, I allowed myself to roll back across the deck with the gybe, decided that if the preventer snapped, there was nothing much I could do about at this stage and concentrated on getting the downhaul on a cleat which didn't already have something else round it.

And then, bit by inexorable bit, I hauled the spinnaker and a good deal of Atlantic into my lap.

By the time everything was squared away, the boat was on course, the household contents were back where they belonged and Maurice was glad he was not young anymore. It was just possible to discern the Eastern horizon. It had been quite a night, I decided. I was looking forward to telling the guys about it on the breakfast time radio schedule.

"I was up all night driving my spinnaker," I told Peter Conole on *Freebird*. We had worked out our positions and *Largo* had gained another 20 miles on him. He sounded impressed. He had spent the night under small genoa alone.

More importantly, that 20 miles difference meant that a couple of days later, he dropped into a calm that never touched me – and that is why the record books show that *Largo's* time was 32 days 21 hours and *Freebird's* 33 days 23 hours.

It is the sort of detail that separates the winners from the losers – or, in this case, the one who came 65th from the one who came 68th.

The Good Stuff – Book One

Chapter 9
Frank Sinatra and the Left-Flanking Movement

They gave us the finisher's plaque before the start. It was a comforting gesture – full of confidence: rather like sending troops into battle with the medals already pinned to their chests.

It was a nice little plaque, too: a plastic tile with AZAB '91 written on it and the boat's name. People would be able to come down into *Largo's* cabin and say: "Ah, you did the Azores and Back."

There was a lot of marina credibility in the plaque.

So why, as soon as I had peeled off the backing strip, did I know that I had done something terribly, terribly wrong?

A shadow passed over the sun. A platoon of departed single-handers tramped over my grave. The boat rocked uncertainly in what ought to have been the calm of Falmouth Harbour.

And, from that moment on, nothing went right.

Take, for instance, the business with the spinnaker: I had spent good money and shed not a few principles in getting a spinnaker squeezer. I was, of course, quite unable to master it and had to listen to Mary Falk (5ft and a smidgeon) explaining: "I haven't used one since I gave up on it and cut the endless line off the Muckle Flugga."

When you think about it, it's worth doing the Round Britain just so you can say something like that.

Sure enough, within two hours of the start, my endless line wrapped itself endlessly round the squeezer – and then the whole lot wrapped endlessly round the forestay.

Ten minutes later, the spinnaker was flying proudly on its own and the squeezer was stuffed in the forepeak, plotting revenge.

This was not long in coming. A hundred miles west of Ushant, the tape player packed up. Now, there may be some skippers in the race who would be fazed by the SatNav going down or the VMG computer churning out numbers for a night at the bingo. But aboard *Largo*, with her new, waterproof cockpit speakers, the greatest disaster imaginable is Frank Sinatra getting halfway through *New York - New*

York and turning into Donald Duck.

This meant switching to the spare tape deck (yes, I carry one) even though it meant some ticklish work with the soldering iron as the boat surfed at 7½ knots.

The following morning was warm and calm, and the saltwater pump in the galley expired. An hour after that, the galley was in the cockpit. That is to say that I had to take the whole sink unit out to get at the pump – and very soggy and smelly it was underneath.

From the log that evening: *1900 Genny down to No3 size, lee rail dipping, and we're bashing on at 5kts+. I don't much want to go out there, and definitely the sextant doesn't, so we'll have to guess where we are. Since it must be more than 250 miles from the nearest land, does it really matter? Anyway, I've set the Decca to look, and it appears to be cruising around the ocean trying out different possibilities like a dog who knows he buried a bone around here somewhere.*

The glass started dropping in a purposeful manner. The mainsheet parted from the end of the boom, and in among the concerto set up by the howl of the wind, the thump of the bow meeting solid water, and the rattle of spray competing with a downpour, there came the small but unmistakable sound of tearing sailcloth.

This would not have happened if I had realised the reefing points should not be tied directly to the dinky little cringles the sailmaker had put in the bottom of the main this year. They promptly went back to the padeyes rivetted to the boom where they belonged.

It was later, lying in my bunk, muttering, that another sound came to me – the sound of a small metal object rolling to and fro on deck. It was a very unnerving sound, conjuring as it did, images of an errant clevis pin.

I looked very hard for this pin. I looked as hard as it is possible to look with a torch through the windows. I looked as thoroughly as anyone could look without actually going out and getting wet. At least I established that the mast was not going to fall down. Indeed, I managed to convince myself that the rattle was really a newly-installed shackle – until now, not a part of the usual noises of the boat at sea.

Wrong. It was the carefully-greased screws undoing themselves from the ends of the new full-length battens and dropping like confetti all over the deck and into the sea.

If you ever want to know what is the point of having a single-sideband radio, it is for moments like this, at the height of a gale, when you can ring up your sailmaker and shout at him.

The sailmaker, of course, recommended a more permanent solution than my idea (which involved lots of string). He wanted holes drilled and bolts inserted. People like that should be given a hand drill and put on a coachroof in the middle of a gale to see how long it takes them to drill through their foot.

By the time I had removed each plastic fitting, taken it below to the vice clamped to the companionway steps, drilled holes for eight tiny bolts, fitted the eight tiny nuts without dropping or swallowing them, I assumed the rest of the fleet was long gone.

As if that was not bad enough, when I looked round, most of the crew had jumped ship: there is a tradition aboard *Largo* that we sail these sorts of races with a geranium aboard. However, after the original died following stalwart service on an AZAB and two transatlantics, friends became over-generous with replacements until the boat began to resemble a large window-box.

Well, not by the end of the gale, she didn't. The pot lashed to the afterdeck simply bailed out over the back, and the one wedged over the galley ended up in misery all over the chart table. The sole survivor went brown and seemed to be growing backwards.

I went into a decline too, and had to be forced to clean up and listen to a lecture on the benefits of the left-flanking movement.

The left-flanking movement is much talked about in AZAB circles, and involves a great sweep down the Portuguese coast, sailing many extra miles but supposedly taking advantage of Portuguese Trades and staying away from the calms of the Azores High until the last possible moment.

At least, that is the theory.

From the log: *Today I resolved not to spend so much time staring at the ocean. Today I resolved to do things.*

I began by getting the light headsail up before breakfast and then doing all the washing up. I spent ten minutes worrying myself sick over a report on the World Service that Alzheimer's Disease is caused by the over-use of aluminium saucepans. I have nothing else.

I even whipped the end of the spinnaker sheet. Am I rewarded for this? Am I, hell. We are now progressing in the wrong direction at 2.4kts. It's that damned plaque. I know it is!

And, of course, it was. For, that was when I did what I should have done all that time ago in Falmouth. I jammed a screwdriver behind the finisher's plaque and wrenched without any thought at all for the damage I might be doing to the bulkhead.

The plaque popped off like a jack-in-the-box and the wind sprang up.

Well, actually, the wind took another 13 hours to spring up, but the two events were undoubtedly connected because, from that moment, everything went right.

I got the trumpet out of its case. This instrument, I have acquired from my 16-year-old son George by the process of premature reverse inheritance and, as *Largo* sailed westwards, I sat with the score of *When the Saints Go Marching In* taped to the cockpit coaming and blew a series of quite different notes.

I have previously maintained that trad jazz – like Vivaldi – attracts dolphins. I should now record that this is not the case. I have no idea why.

After all, when I sailed into Ponta Delgada, last of the fleet after 14 days and met *Castaway*, the Freedom 35 motoring off for a picnic because they'd been there so long, I gave them a rendition, and they were good enough to applaud.

Even so, I suppose the early lessons might explain the lack of a pigeon. Everyone else seemed to give a lift to a racing pigeon. The most spectacular was Charlie, who signed on with the Condor 37 *Sally May* within sight of Land's End and practically walked ashore at the other end. Two days after they got in, he was still strutting up and down the pontoon, looking for his muesli.

Robert Nickerson, the skipper of the 60ft *Panic Major* took a rather different view of his passenger. Robert is a farmer and tends not to get sentimental about livestock: "The wretched thing had three days' warning. By the time it was 480 miles further from land than when it arrived, and my crew came down saying he couldn't get a grip on deck because of the mess, I took a winch handle to it. Its owner would have wrung its neck, anyway; nothing more useless than a lazy racing pigeon."

It was quite a topic of conversation while the fleet was in – that and what happened to everyone's laundry.

The last of my smalls arrived half an hour before the restart – along with another commemorative plaque, this one presented by the Clube Naval. I hid it in the galley locker and *Largo* started with an unexpected lucky break. As one of only four boats to take the eastern - and meteorologically more dicey - route round the island, we carried the wind all the way and ended up careering along under too big a spinnaker, mostly out of control and with the log occasionally claiming 8.9 knots.

And this went on... and on. After three days, the overall average was an unheard-of 5.3 knots. I began to think that the family wedding I had felt rather guilty in refusing might be a possibility after all. I crammed on all sail. I did things like getting up in the middle of the night to change spinnakers.

We chafed through the guy, it was up for so long. We pulled the clew out (and spent a whole evening sewing it back in).

When a gale roared up on the tail, I strapped down two reefs and a poled-out jib and stood in the hatch mesmerised by the scene as a huge full moon lit up a monochrome seascape with waves blown flat and long streaks of spume stretching all the way to the horizon.

I did not, as it happens, get to the wedding. In fact, we crossed the finishing line in Falmouth an hour before the bride reached the altar in Newbury.

Largo had managed to cover the 1,200 miles in 8 days 22hours 56minutes. That was faster than the old record. It was so fast that, on the return leg, we won on handicap.

I would stick the plaque up again, but - come the prizegiving - there might be something more spectacular to occupy that space on the bulkhead.

The Good Stuff – Book One

Chapter 10
The Anchor and How to Survive It

Deep in the subconscious, nature's alarm clock sounded.

It is possible that the insistent drumming of the rain on the coachroof, the slap of the growing waves on the hull or the slightly rising note of wind in the rigging might all have woken me. Any one of them would have been as effective as a shout from the cockpit.

But it is much more impressive to think that I was somehow in tune with the infinite.

Anyway, it was about three in the morning; we were anchored off Pottery Pier, that northern tip of Brownsea Island in Poole Harbour, when I decided I had better get up and have a look.

Actually, I do this with absurd regularity. I wake up, I assume there must be a reason for it (usually an impressive, subconscious one), and I heave myself out of the sleeping bag and go and stand in the hatch wondering what the devil I'm doing there.

It's hereditary, of course. My father was a great one for stumbling about in the middle of the night, waking us all up and then announcing: "Just checking the warps," as if, without him, we would have ended up in Fernando Po.

He did it once when we were the inside boat of a trot that went halfway across a Dutch canal. His weight in the cockpit turned out to be the equivalent of the last straw breaking the camel's back – in this case, popping the stern cleat out of the deck and risking the entire raft of boats spinning off into the Ijsselmeer.

He said it was lucky he got up just when he did. I always contend that he would have done better to stay in bed.

Anyway, the result for me is that, as soon as the brain switches back on and registers that it is still the middle of the night, I am gripped by the blinding realisation that *something* needs my attention – and needs it *immediately*.

It never does, of course. Never, that is, except for that night in Poole. I stood in the hatch and witnessed two dozen boats all leaving the anchorage at once. The anchor lights were moving ahead *en masse* – as if someone had appointed themselves admiral and hoisted a signal.

In which case, why had no one told me? Why had I been left to sleep through the storm, or the attack by French privateers or whatever it was that was coming?

"*Largo!*" shouted a voice from out of the darkness. "*Largo,* you're dragging!"

And, good heavens, so we were. Thinking about it later, this was a much more obvious explanation than the mass evacuation. It was not so much that everyone else was going forwards. The problem was that I was going backwards.

The incident also demonstrates why it is a very good idea to have the boat's name written down both sides of the hull in big letters. Anyway, reality took hold of the situation, and I padded up to the foredeck and put a hand on the anchor chain. Sure enough, it trembled with that uncannily clear vibration which seems able to travel undiminished up no many how many fathoms of chain.

In fact, it was vibrating so much that it gave a clear impression of the anchor bouncing and tumbling its way across the seabed on some mission of its own.

I took a look behind to see where we were going to end up and saw a trim little 23footer nodding quietly in the wind. *Largo* is a Rival 32ft and a bit of a lump sometimes. She has a bow like a banana which the wind catches and slams from side to side like a barn door. The prospect of her arriving uninvited alongside her neighbour was too embarrassing to contemplate.

Standing there on the foredeck with my Mark's & Spencer's pyjamas whipping about me, I veered another couple of fathoms of cable. This time, when the wind took hold of the bow, the chain yanked it back with a vicious tug that practically had me over the side.

This was all very well, but we were almost back on the little guy behind. Certainly, there was no longer any room to drag again, and if the positions had been reversed, I would have felt very peeved that someone had anchored so close. Obviously, I had to move.

Starting up the engine, I hauled *Largo* up to her anchor again, broke it out and then, as that great bow swung off the wind, nipped smartly back to the cockpit, wrestled the gear lever into forward (it was of a certain vintage and always a bit of a battle) and revved the throttle.

At once, I knew that something was wrong. The engine responded like a turbo-charged Porsche. It felt as if I was sitting at traffic lights, trying to frighten old ladies towing wicker shopping baskets. We were not in gear.

More to the point, we were now across the wind and going down fast on our little neighbour. Back up on the foredeck where the chain was still dumped in a heap, I slung the hook out again and shovelled all those fathoms after it.

I let us slide back until we were about 6ft off the little guy's bow and slightly to one side. At this point, something must have stirred in the other skipper's subconscious – for a head appeared in the hatch, looking in the other direction, of course. I watched it turn round like a mechanical toy. I watched the mouth fall open, and I swear I caught the flash of the whites of the eyes as the situation dawned.

"Sorry," I called, the word carrying easily on the wind. The head in the hatch jabbered soundlessly for some minutes.

"I've been dragging, and now I have engine trouble," I explained as if the combination were the sort of thing that could happen to anyone. "It would be best if you could drop back a bit until I can fix it. Is that OK?"

The head ducked down and emerged a minute or two later. Underneath it was a yellow oilskin jacket and a pair of long spindly white legs. The skipper came up to his foredeck where we could have talked if he had felt like it. Instead, he busied himself letting out another three or four fathoms and then scuttled back to his hatch where he crouched, watching for further developments.

Since *Largo* seemed to be staying put and disasters, of all kinds, were gradually receding, I grabbed a couple of handfuls of assorted tools and disappeared head-first into the back of the engine – an intriguing manoeuvre aboard *Largo* since it involves tunnelling under the quarter berth.

There, in the oily darkness, it transpired that nuts had loosened, cables had been slipping, and there were various other simple explanations for complicated disasters, all of which could have been avoided with a little basic maintenance.

Wriggling out backwards, red in the face from upside-down exertion, I started the engine, noted the satisfying vibration as the propeller bit into the water and motored ahead so that I could haul in chain by the armful, dropping it in a great clattering heap on deck before we fell back again.

Carefully, I took us back to where we should have been in the first place, lined us up head to wind and set the anchor with all the deliberation of the Queen Mother casting for salmon on the Dee.

Largo settled obediently. I gave the engine a good long rev in reverse to dig us in and then switched off and took a contented look around. The man on the little boat was still up, so I gave him a wave. He continued to stare at me as if I was mad. I shivered and went below.

There, I was surprised to find a small figure in a smaller pair of Mark's & Spencer's pyjamas who swayed with more than the motion of the boat.

My son Olly, then aged no more than 10: I had forgotten all about him. He squinted in the light and demanded: "What's going on?"

He had been asleep in the fo'c'sle. All that chain hitting the deck not 3ft above his head, and only now had he woken up. His younger brother was still asleep with that utterly carefree expression children have when lying on their backs with their small clenched fists thrown over their heads.

"Nothing to worry about," I told Olly, tucking him back into his sleeping bag. The other touching thing about children of that age is that they have such utter faith. They really believe their father knows what he's doing.

How could I tell them he doesn't – or, at least, not when it comes to anchoring. For a start, none of this might have happened if I had known what the marks on the chain meant. They were ingeniously chosen so that each one felt different in the dark: There would be a strand of polypropylene tied through a link, then a length of codline. After that came braided terylene and then more polypropylene – but frayed this time.

It would have been marvellous if only the previous owner had written it down as soon as he invented it. From time to time, I tried to make sense of it. Did the polypropylene mark ten feet or two fathoms – or were we in metres?

You would think that, after nine years, I would have worked it out, but no; with the anchor, I have a mental block – just as I have a mental block with speed limits. As soon as the depth recorder goes down to 10ft and I stick the bow in among a gaggle of anchored boats, a great unease creeps over me. Every little bit of water has something wrong with it – this one is a bit too near that boat; that one is over this boat's chain. There are wind-rode motor cruisers to be considered, lightweight racing machines on 10mm nylon warp ready to bounce around like conkers on pieces of elastic…

Show me a piece of flat, untroubled water, and I will see sunken piles underneath – with sharpened points. Suggest we actually drop the anchor sometime, and I will take us round on another circuit of the bay like a wet-biker trying to make friends.

Of course, I didn't start out well when it comes to anchors. The first time I anchored for the night and actually went to sleep was in an 18ft Caprice in the lee of Hurst Castle. Solent Yachtsmen will already be sucking their teeth at the suggestion. The tide in the lee of Hurst Castle is somewhat eccentric. You only have to look at the eddies and breakers all over the place to know that, while it might be fine for lunch, it does not qualify as a secure anchorage – certainly not if you only have a couple of fathoms of chain and the rest is rope.

The essence of the problem is that if the yacht and her anchor are more than 10ft apart, the one will behave without any reference to the other, and the rope will wander off looking for trouble. I awoke in the morning to find the warp bar-taut and leading diagonally down the topsides to enter the water somewhere level with the companionway. This seemed an odd place for it to go.

Peering beneath the surface – something you can do in a Caprice without getting out – it became apparent that, during the night, the tide had been walking us round in circles so that now the anchor warp was twice round the bilge keels. I had to undo the bitter end and walk twice round the deck in the opposite direction.

There was another time when, feeling rather pleased about having got to Brittany, and anchoring next to the only other boat in the lower reaches of Jaudy river, just down from Treguier, the anchor disappeared straight down, taking the whole 60ft of warp with it and hung there, mocking me.

This had never happened before. I mean, where, on this side of the Channel, do you anchor in more than 60ft of water? I tied a mooring warp onto the end … and then another … and then the spare sheets. Finally, we were anchored on the end of about 200ft of line. Now I know how a Yorkshire terrier feels on the end of one of those extendable dog leads.

Of course, little *Amicus* did not have much of an anchor – 20lbs was plenty – and the kedge was a featherweight 10lbs. You didn't have to row it out when you went aground; you just whirled it around a bit and threw it like a cowboy roping a steer.

Most cowboys, though, do not have to have to face the problem of a botched knot coming undone in mid-flight and the anchor with its 6ft of chain, flying freely through the air and disappearing comprehensively under the water. I had to go over the side and tramp around until I stubbed my toe on it.

Oh, the troubles there have been over anchors – anchors under mooring ground chains, anchors sliding gently through the ooze so that each morning the boat is a little further back and every few days, we have to motor up and start again. Anchors that won't come up again…

This is a particular problem on boats without a windlass and singlehanded boats, the more so. In fact, since back trouble has been identified as one of the primary causes of lost working days in Britain, it might not be a bad idea for the government to lift VAT on windlasses.

Of course, with a little ingenuity, there is no need for a windlass. The system works like this: pull up the cable until the backbone begins to creak. Make fast and motor forward to a spot approximately over the anchor. Pull in until the second and third lumbar vertebrae become impacted. Make fast and nip back to the cockpit to motor forward again. Repeat this performance two or three times until either the anchor breaks out, or the backbone does.

In the latter case, a last resort is to put the engine in reverse and stretch back on the cable rather like a pebble in a catapult. When she won't go back anymore, charge ahead over the top of the anchor – and hold on…

If you are able to drag the bow under water without shifting the anchor, the chances are it is fouled, and you will have to go down there and reason with it. This is a lot easier in a Pacific lagoon than an English river where you can't see a hand in front of your face, and the obstruction is 3ft down in the mud.

So why put up with it? Why not go, as so many people do go, from one convenient, sanitised marina berth to another.

I believe it has something to do with the fact that the process of anchoring is one of the few things about boats which is essentially unchanged since the days of the Vikings.

Lie to an anchor, and you are directly in touch with all those sailors who have gone before, who lay in their bunks or their hammocks, or on sheepskins on top of stone ballast and listened to the moaning of the wind and the creak of the cable – and knew they could never completely relax.

Chapter 11
Going Slowly

Dogwatch began with three or four short pieces on the page – that was before I realised that the hard part for a columnist is thinking of something to write about. The easy part is spinning it out to fill the space.

This may explain a lot: I think the best part of ocean racing is going slowly.

It is not to deny the mind-scrambling frustration of falling into a hole and watching impotently as the rest of the fleet pound off to the horizon – nor should we ignore that spirit-lifting sensation of a spinnaker filled with a steady Force 5 while the miles tick off hour by hour.

But some of the most memorable times have been spent sitting in the cockpit, chin on the coaming, watching the bubbles crawl past so slowly that each one gets examined individually while tiny bugs appear from nowhere to skitter about on the surface, engaged in frantic business of their own.

At times like this, when an old-fashioned logline hangs straight down and its electronic counterpart conjures 0.1kts out of little more than goodwill, the world seems to stand still. The silence broken only by the occasional gurgle of a skin fitting and the creak of the boom as a long, low swell passes underneath on its way to somewhere else.

Then there is nothing to be done. Once the crew accepts that the race for them, is temporarily suspended. They stop tweaking at the sheets and waggling at the tiller. The idea of getting out the dinghy oars and rowing is consigned to that repository of idiotic suggestions where it belongs – all that is left is lapse into companionable silence and enjoy the moment.

It never seems to happen in a cruising boat. There is always some sort of urgency to turn on the engine and "get there".

In a race, around the buoys, when the rest of the fleet is still within sight – or even within swearing distance – it is the competitive spirit that gets in the way.

But a few hundred miles out in the ocean, with the finishing line a matter of weeks away rather than hours, all sorts of things take on a different perspective.

This is not the way to win, of course – but it does make a fine excuse for coming last.

Chapter 12
Wash Day Blues

They call it progress - in the same way they call telescopic boathooks progress - but somewhere along the line, somebody decided that quality of life could be measured by the number of washing machines per head of population – and laundrettes started to disappear.

Time was, when you could arrive anywhere that had a pub and a post office and find the Quay Laundrette or the Harbour Washeteria next door. It was always busy, filled with local gossip - which promptly died as the yachtie's duffle bag spilled out onto the floor with a damp and musty flop, and a million mildew spores made their break for freedom.

But now that every home has its Hotpoint, someone has turned the Seaview Laundromat into Quay Amusements; if you put 10p in the slot, you get terminated by Arnold Schwarzenegger. No more, the innocent pleasure of trying to get the cup under the powder dispenser before the enzymes hit the floor.

Of course, the glossier marinas have installed laundry rooms - at a ratio of one machine to 600 berths. But the dockmaster can give directions to the last laundrette in town - even if that is uphill all the way and usually in the rain.

Meanwhile, the French, who are even more proud of their standard of living, take matters to extremes. It may be that the sight of T-shirts and smalls on the guardrails is as much a part of the summer cruise as oysters and Muscadet, but last year we made the mistake of setting off without first taking a good sniff at the bedding.

By Tréguier, the fo'c'sle was an embarrassment. We were beginning to worry about spreading the sleeping bags on the boom to air – particularly upwind of anyone else.

In the *Laverie*, two huge and belligerent women behind a rampart of bundles insisted that nothing could be touched for two days.

Plouman'ach turned out to not to have a laundrette at all (no matter what the book said), and by the time we arrived at Morlaix and wheeled a supermarket trolley of unpleasantness through the streets like a Trojan horse, we were in no mood at all for the sign on the door which greeted us: "Closed indefinitely due to family tragedy."

There was very nearly another one.

Chapter 13
Bright Eyes?

When the windspeed indicator hits 35 knots, and the boat takes on the characteristics of a fairground whirligig, there is a lot to be said for sitting still.

I was sitting very still, tucked under the sprayhood, one foot braced against the leeward cockpit seat and with the autopilot taking the solid water sluicing down the side deck.

We were on our way from Gosport to Honfleur and had already decided against running for Littlehampton for various good and seamanlike reasons, including the fact that Littlehampton is just not the same as Honfleur for a long weekend.

So we tucked the second reef down and wound up the genny until it was about the size of a Sainsbury's carrier bag - and setting about as well.

The mate rolled herself up in a sleeping bag on the lee berth while the skipper settled heroically to the long night watch, staying awake with Art Garfunkel playing on the cockpit speakers.

The secret, of course, is not just to sit still hour after hour until you drift into a state which you can fool yourself is wakefulness. The secret is to do things – to take in that third reef the moment you think of it … to deal with the signal halyard when it first begins to come undone, not when it's streaming out horizontally from the crosstrees.

But I never did find the energy to change the tape. Art Garfunkel auto-reversed backwards and forwards every 25 minutes for a solid ten hours.

I'd rather face another gale than listen to *Bright Eyes* again.

Chapter 14
Seadog Trials

We have a boat dog. At least, we hope we have a boat dog.

He hates the water, but that may yet prove a bonus – pulling them out when they're wet and surprised is never easy.

I used to know a boat dog who could climb ladders – going down again was another matter and entailed his master standing in the dinghy, holding out his long oilskin coat. The dog would launch himself from the quay, and the two of them would land in a heap on the bottom boards.

My parents, if they had given any thought to it, would never have chosen a dachshund to take on a Folkboat. Henry was 18inches long and *Torgunn's* decks were 12 inches wide. If he set off from the cockpit, he had no choice but to go all the way round.

Then we had Beau, a cocker spaniel with fur that clogged the pumps and absolutely no idea where the hard stopped and the mud started at Pin Mill.

And now Blue has come into my life. He looks like the very picture of a boat dog, a mongrel like the ones in the old barge prints. He'll present a marvellous profile standing on the foredeck, sniffing the air as we drift up the river on the evening flood, gin in hand, at peace with the world.

We introduced him to *Largo* one winter weekend, just to see what he would make of it – no point in investing in a dog harness until we knew if he liked it. So we improvised with one of his towels, cutting two holes for his front legs and tying it in two huge knots on his back. He looked as though he was wearing a nappy.

"We're seeing if he's a boat dog," we explained to bystanders as we heaved him into the launch in the manner of Hornblower's livestock being swayed aboard.

John, the boatman, took in the wild, rolling eyes, the four legs all straining for the ground and announced: "You're wasting your time." But an hour later, the new boat dog was picking his way around *Largo's* deck, sniffing appreciatively at seagull droppings. Come the summer, he'll be up there on the foredeck, ears cocked, tail like a flag, looking forward to his run ashore.

Meanwhile, does anyone know where I can get a long oilskin coat?

Chapter 15
Bumps In the Night

We called them the Colonel and his Lady. They were probably nothing of the kind, but he stood ramrod straight, and she seemed to be permanently on the point of offering sherry.

They were ensconced in Plouman'ach and appeared to have been there for some time. They had a 'gentleman's motor yacht' – no chrome or tinted glass but two thumping great diesels and all the right flags.

We were just about to come alongside and wondering how to scale the cliff-like bulwarks when the Colonel popped his head out of the wheelhouse, bursting with apologies, and suggested we try his other side. "Feller who was here last night – nice chap – about your size – found it a bit shallow – try the other side – my advice…"

And so we did. They took our lines and chatted amiably. They were living aboard for the summer, something they had always planned to do although, as she said: "You finally manage it, and then you die; that's the awful thing."

Not just then, of course. Instead, she politely bustled off and left us to ourselves. A delightful couple, we decided, and so helpful. They quite made us review our prejudices about people with motorboats.

We were still thinking along these lines – if we thought anything at all – when, at about two in the morning, a roll of Sellotape fell off the chart table. Odd, that; it was calm in the entirely protected harbour. In fact, it was very calm indeed, so calm that the boat seemed to have acquired a curious sort of solidity, almost as if she were part of the land rather than the sea.

I rolled over to go back to sleep. It was very easy to roll over. In fact, I had just reached that comfortable state of semi-consciousness when everything else fell off the chart table in an extended, if slightly hesitant, avalanche. Two pencils, the almanac, a bag of plums and Jilly Coopers' latest bonkbuster hit the floor one after the other with a sort of languorous crescendo that defied sleep.

It was Tamsin whose mind managed to grasp the explanation first: "We're aground," she said.

At least, that was what she tried to say. With the pair of us piled in a heap against the lockers, speech was a muffled business. I scrambled out and looked: The moon glistened on large expanses of mud and weed. The warps groaned. Somewhere in my mind, there danced the vision of cleats popping out of the deck like champagne corks – or possibly the motor yacht sedately toppling over and crushing us. I began to scuttle about the deck stark naked, easing things.

The clinometer on the compass pushed past 20°, and then 30. Down below, the lockers became the berth. Tamsin crawled around the side of the boat, rearranging her bed through a right angle. There was another creak, another round of easing warps. I was running out of rope. 40°...

The bilge water crept out from under the cabin sole and met the clothes which had slipped quietly off the settee berth. Things fell out of racks separately and at two-minute intervals. It was like living with a very lazy poltergeist.

I fished the almanac out of the soggy pile under the galley and looked up the tide tables. This was going to go on for another hour. It would be another three before we came remotely upright again.

For want of anything else to think about, I decided that we had grounded on a hump. Gradually the hump grew in detail, and the boat up-ended on it. If real-life went the way of the nightmare, then eventually, the mast would dip below the horizontal. When the tide rose again, Largo would fill with water as surely as a watering can dipped into a garden pond. I could see us climbing up the warps to save ourselves.

Going on deck was like working in a state of permanent broach. Amidships, the tow-rail was under water. I poked about with an oar and found the bottom. At least it was there. We would not be going any further.

And sure enough, somewhere around four in the morning, Largo began to come up again. The dawn arrived, silhouetting Plouman'ach's peculiar rock formations against the grey in the east. The crew's spirits began to lift as well. After all, there was nothing more to be done; The springs – living up to their name – would settle us back in position. It was time to get some sleep.

A good deal of thought went into this and a certain amount of trial and error. We ended up head to tail. Like sardines in a heavy and unromantic embrace, we lay there and listened while our world slowly rolled back into place again.

By breakfast time, things looked surprisingly normal. The harbour was full of water once more; the muddy stain on Largo's topsides was drying to a crust, and as on every other day of his life, the Colonel came to his door and sniffed the air. Then he asked pleasantly: "Comfortable night?"

Chapter 16
The Jet Skier Solution

The sound seemed to come from a long way away, cutting through the dream-like haze laid down by the last bottle of rosé from St Vaast. It was the sound of a chain saw or maybe a small motorbike.

For a while, I lay there, staring at the inside of my hat and wondering which. The truth finally dawned when the snarling reached a crescendo, the slap of high-speed wash hit the hull, and the boat gave one of those desultory lurches that remind you of a bored horse.

I lifted the hat and just managed to catch a glimpse of my first jet skier. Up and down he went, snarling and revving, banking sharply to cut across his own wake, the engine screaming a banshee note which slammed through the anchorage like an Exocet.

Hurling my hat onto the cockpit sole, I stood up, hands on hips, lower lip to the fore, outrage at the ready.

What happened? The moron in the wetsuit decided he had an appreciative audience. He did a lap of honour.

Grinning and waggling his neoprene bottom, he circled for approval. What he got was a torrent of abuse, but it didn't make any difference. He couldn't hear a thing.

But that was all a few years ago. Since then, in the manner of a landowner discovering a hippy commune in the water meadow, I have made a few enquiries. The important thing to understand, apparently, is that jet ski riders are "water users".

For somebody who always thought a water user was anyone with a washing machine, this was worrying news. Apparently, we are all water users. The yachtsman with his faded Breton cap and lifetime's understanding of wind on tide has no more right to use the water than some XR3i driver looking for a new thrill.

The harbourmaster commiserated. He supposed that most of them knew as much about the rules-of-the-road as they did about the azimuth of Polaris, but as long as they kept out of the way of the ferry and obeyed the speed limit in the river, there was precious little he could do about them.

I began shaking my fist when they roared past. I shouted abuse, but it was like asking the Hell's Angels if they wouldn't mind being a little quieter, please.

The noise is part of the fun. It is essential to the display. After all, would the Red Arrows be half as thrilling if they shot past at treetop height and broke into a starburst of multi-coloured smoke, all in total silence?

No, the jet-skier has to telegraph his presence with his wasp-like snarl so that everyone stops and stares. Only then can he launch into his routine: round and round and backwards and forwards - and then the same thing all over again.

He smiles broadly. His friends join him. They jump over each other's wakes. Their engines scream. They are, - at least until they run out of petrol - artists of horsepower and balance. If anybody has a waterproof pen, they will sign autographs.

The one thing they will not do is stop.

For a long time, I pondered this. I dreamed of sabotage, the old potato up the exhaust pipe trick or treacle in the purple bootees. But in the end, it was human nature which provided the answer.

I waited for a particularly troublesome one to perform his most intricate feat of snarling and pirouetting and then I stood on the side deck and waved both hands above my head.

Like John Wayne on a cattle drive, he reared his machine round in a tight turn and came storming back. Maybe somebody was in trouble. Maybe he could perform some selfless act of skill and bravery - possibly ferry a small and photogenic child to hospital in the nick of time…

Swinging round in a foaming arc, he slowed and beamed hopefully under his plastic fluorescent crash helmet.

I called to him, but very quietly indeed.

Frowning, he cut the throttle altogether, which meant that he stopped dead in the water and had no choice but to fall off.

I muttered even more earnestly, but what with his engine idling right by his ear, the poor fellow was still unable to hear. He pulled a switch, and instantly, blissful silence closed in from all sides.

We looked at each other across three or four yards of increasingly calm water, and then, in no more than a pleasant conversational tone, I said: "Peaceful, when you turn it off, isn't it?"

―――――――

Chapter 17
Jimmy the One

The boat was built like a tank. With hull plating in 5mm steel, a cockpit the size of a bucket and flush decks designed to be continually swept by breaking seas, she had been designed with one purpose in mind: to go storming round the world, knocking aside floating containers, icebergs and any notion that sailing might be a form of relaxation.

Of course, I blame myself. I remember standing once with Jimmy, the skipper, on the quay at Wivenhoe and looking at the boats.

"Do you think I could learn to sail?" said Jimmy.

"Why not? A lot of other people did – and besides, he already knew about boats. He was a prodigious fisherman. He used to take an inflatable miles out into the Thames Estuary and lay longlines with 250 hooks. Jimmy never did anything by halves.

The following spring, he bought himself a 26 footer and sailed it up and down the Essex coast as if he were trying to compress the circumference of the globe into the space between the Swale and Orfordness.

He sailed all the winter too. I went to join him one February morning. When he opened the hatch, I was hit by a blast of superheated air as if he was living in a brick kiln.

"Standing charge for the electricity," explained Jimmy, shirtless. "Might as well use it."

He had kept the fan heater going all night.

In the clubhouse, people used to gather behind the picture windows to watch him – a frenetic figure in his oilskins setting out into weather which made older members forego the ice in their gin.

Incorrigible was the word that came to mind. Within a few years, he had moved up to 32ft and was getting even more serious. Not only did he learn to use a sextant, but he turned sight reduction into a kind of race. Eventually, he was producing a position line in something absurd like 76 seconds – all very creditable, but where on earth was the point?

The point, explained Jimmy, was that in among the coral reefs of the Tuamotus group, it was entirely possible that such swift Astro-navigation would be vital.

It was the same with the hydraulic steering - enough pounds per square inch to put the gunwale under on the QEII. Then there were the seacocks – all above the waterline, sitting like birds on the top of tall steel pipes so that, even if the ship burned down, she would still float.

The whole project was being undertaken with a seriousness befitting a polar expedition, and it left the same uneasy sense of foreboding – for, amid all this preparation, one thing appeared to have been thrown together without a moment's thought – the crew.

It was almost as if Jimmy had taken them on like the rest of the stores: one gallon of Stockholm tar; two foredeck hands; case of tinned tomatoes; engineer/rigger.

Far more voyages have been wrecked by fractured personal relationships that ever came to grief on coral reefs.

Even happily married couples find it difficult: I know of one pair who had lived contentedly on land for 30 years and then spent the day sulking at opposite ends of a Sadler 34 because he wanted to turn the engine on, and she didn't.

Another husband arrived in Falmouth at the end of a passage from The Azores, unable to hide the shame of 15ft of shredded spinnaker flying from the masthead like a windsock because his wife had refused to let him climb the mast to retrieve it.

And sure enough, by the time Jimmy and his crew arrived in the Med, the personalities were grating like the gears on a Tunisian bus.

Looking back on it now, Jimmy blames the man who squeezed the toothpaste in the middle - and the one who insisted they sail back from Majorca to Malaga because his daughter was coming out for a holiday, and that was where the cheapest flights went.

The skipper should have taken this as a warning. On the day of the girl's arrival, the crew set out for the airport, argued about the cost of a taxi, the heat and each other – and all walked off in different directions.

The boat sat in marinas around the western Mediterranean for more than a year with a For Sale sign hanging in the rigging.

As for Jimmy, he has opted for solitude – but again, not by halves. Now he lives in a lighthouse keeper's cottage in the Hebrides.

Chapter 18
Tacking the Dog

The boat dog put his paws up on the gunwale and sniffed the salt air appreciatively. This was what he had been waiting for. This is what we had been waiting for. Ever since I introduced Blue, wrapped in a towel and being swayed aboard like Hornblower's cattle, this black Labrador cross of such doubtful parentage that the term "mongrel" is a positive compliment, has achieved an alarming celebrity status.

"So this is the famous boat dog," people said as they found him sniffing his way round the boatyard when *Largo* came out for her scrub.

When we bought him a lifejacket, he swaggered around the pontoons as if he were modelling Armani instead of Crewsaver. Maybe he would turn out to be a born boat dog.

We took him for a Sunday sail to see how he measured up. You might have thought the fuss in the Solent was all for him rather than the returning BT Challenge fleet. As we slipped out of Portsmouth harbour on a gentle reach, he sat there on the windward deck with his tongue out, positively basking in all the attention as everyone we passed smiled and exclaimed and pointed.

And then, with the world-weary air of one who has seen it all and forgotten most of it, the boat dog languorously crossed his front legs, laid his nose on top of them and went to sleep. Surreptitiously, we opened the ham salad rolls and toasted his success with last year's Kronenbourg.

At this point, anyone who knows anything about boats – or, indeed, anything about dogs – could forgive themselves for muttering something about a "false sense of security". And very rightly too – because sometime, we were going to have to turn round.

It happened midway between wondering where the massed fleet of spectator boats had got to and peering through binoculars at four irritatingly identical masts side by side in Ocean Village Marina. Sure enough, half the fleet had found the tidal gates up the Channel wide open for them, and the other half were still being high-minded and philosophical off St Alban's Head and would not be in before nightfall. So we gybed and began the long beat back against the tide.

And that was how we learned about tacking the dog.

This is not a manoeuvre you will find in the sailing manuals but, after a good deal of trial and error, I suggest the most efficient system goes like this.

Depth recorder reading 2.5metres: Look around, mainsheet traveller to leeward, dog to cockpit.

Ready about: Ease the sheet, dog's front fee to leeward seat.

Lee-oh: Dog's front feet to side deck. Back fee to cockpit seat. Let fly the sheet.

Yacht settles on new tack: Furious winching. Dog wanders up side deck, settles against coachroof. Crew grunt over last turn of winch. Dog yawns.

Of course, it does not always happen like this. There is, for instance, the variation of: (a) Dog's tail laid across mainsail track. (b) Dog puts all four feet in coils of headsail sheet. (c) Dog gest three feet out of the cockpit and then tries to get back in again.

But generally speaking, it went well enough – at least it did until the ferry went past.

Now, *Largo* being a Rival, is a dry boat. She does not take much water on deck. However, she must have hit the ferry's wash awkwardly because a dollop of Solent came aboard and landed with astonishing accuracy right on top of the dozing dog. Not having the slightest idea where it had come from, he did what any sensible dog would do and retreated – although, since he happened to be facing aft, that meant backing up towards the bow.

The second wave caught him right in his dignity. He stood there dripping and quivering and gave us the kind of look that suggested he had gone off the whole idea, that we were heartless and cruel, and as soon as he got ashore, he would be calling Dogline to set Esther Rantzen on us.

We could hardly blame him. On the other hand, once he had dried out and discovered all that salt to be licked off, he was back up there looking for all the world as if he had lived his life afloat.

Now all we need really is a bigger boat - one with a cockpit large enough for four pairs of feet and a tail

———————

Chapter 19
The Staff of Life

"Knives," said Adrian Donovan, when asked to name the most useless piece of equipment aboard *Heath Insured* in the British Steel Challenge.

Not the lockspike and lanyard variety, you understand, but the table knife – as in knives and forks.

As in table service.

As in that glorious moment when the whole crew sits down together round the saloon table to celebrate a successful passage: Bacon and eggs with all the trimmings, the cook's signature stroganoff with duchess potatoes and the last of the asparagus – Brie that drips onto a fresh baguette...

Proper food.

Because food and boats are inseparable pleasures – and the idea of sailing round the world the wrong way on a diet of freeze-dried, rehydrated goo is, shall we say, an acquired pleasure. Or, to put it another way, crazy.

Now, I may never have won a race in my life, but if they were awarding prizes for gastronomy at sea, I would be up there with Chittenden and Blake and the rest.

Racing two-handed from Crossshaven to Morgat, we took on extra stewing steak for six. The first night out, a forecast Force 4-5 turned into 7-8, and *Largo* roared off at hull speed, surfing down rollers which had taken 3,000 miles to get themselves organised. As each one passed under the keel, the helmsman brought the tiller up to his chin, and the cook eyed the pressure cooker rather in the manner of a bomb disposal expert counting to ten.

But, taking it in turns, with feet braced against the settee opposite, we sat down to that stew for dinner - and then lunch the next day and finally, as the Ushant light beckoned from the port bow and the wind eased, we polished it off with a degree of decorum in the cockpit.

The dish improved with age. Maybe it was fermenting – or perhaps being bucketed around for 48 hours had the effect of continual stirring.

Yet, there were people who reached the finishing line after us who staggered ashore, gaunt and hungry after trying to sustain themselves on digestive biscuits.

"Too rough to cook," they said.

It is never too rough to cook – although there have been times when cooking has become a little messy.

It was a mistake, for instance, to decide on fresh bread mid-way through the 1988 OSTAR just as a wind shift set up an infuriating slop that jerked us about like a pretty painted sailing boat on a nursery mobile when somebody opens the window.

There is a stage in mixing dough when part of the contents of the bowl has the consistency of wet cement, and the rest is as dry as dust.

And that, sure enough, was the stage at which it slipped off the engine casing and stuck itself to the front of my clean trousers – just washed, as I remember, after my previous culinary discovery (spaghetti Bolognese on a plate in a beam sea).

I suppose the reason I was still out there while Philippe Poupon was crossing the line had something to do with all this – and, of course, the biltong.

This haunch of air-dried South African beef had been hanging up and hitting me in the eye for 1,500 miles. Every time I carved a bit off it and started chewing, it still tasted somewhere between raw Oxo cube and rotten floorboard.

However, sometime before the drying process, it must have started out as prime South African rump, so I reasoned that nothing could be lost by reversing the process. I tried soaking it.

There is, of course, a law that says liquid finds its own level and, after two days, I stopped mopping the galley floor. After three, a strange organic smell began to emanate from the bilges.

The actual cooking took some four or five hours with periodic additions of each and every herb and spice on the boat, most of the condiments and even the contents of the unmarked pot which might possibly have been something to do with the engine.

It is true that the meat still had the consistency of floorboards – albeit softened by a leaking washing machine – but the gravy was something that would have brought a smile to the lips of Escoffier.

And the fact that it looked exactly like pre-packed, freeze-dried, rehydrated E-numbers and was eaten directly out of the saucepan with a wooden spoon is entirely beside the point.

Chapter 20
Boat Time

It was a steel cable – about the size of a child's wrist – and it stretched from the dredger on one side of the approach to Honfleur to a stout bollard on the far bank, and *Largo* was approaching it at her full six knots with absolutely no possibility of stopping in time.

Obviously, there had to be a reason for this – in fact, looking back on it, there was a whole range of reasons. None of them was particularly valid in its own right, but together, they contrived to produce a weight of argument capable of unhinging even the most reasonable mind.

There was the fact that we had set out from Deauville with the intention of arriving in time for the first lock; there was the matter of the grey sky and the cold headwind that made us decide to motor-sail and get it over with, and then there was the business of cutting inside the first couple of buoys to make up time – and finally, the slamming forward of the throttle because we thought we might still just have a chance of getting in before the lock gates slammed shut…

So, the result was that even though we knew we were a full ten minutes late and the boats coming out were streaming past while we still had 300 yards to go… nevertheless, we careered round the final bend with the engine screaming and a bow-wave fit for a pilot boat.

I began to come down to earth when I saw the first Frenchman making "slow down" gestures.

And, while there was no excuse for the gesture from the fisherman tied up against the far wall, why were so many people shouting?

It was at about this point that I saw the cable. It was 40ft ahead, and somebody was lowering it as fast as an ancient and unseen winch could unwind. With a strangled cry, I slammed the gear lever into reverse and was rewarded with the sort of noise which makes people in the middle distance wince.

Imperceptibly, *Largo* slowed. Imperceptibly, the cable sank into the water a millisecond before we shot over the top of it.

What on earth had we been thinking?

We asked ourselves this very question as we tied up at the waiting jetty, and the sun came out. We sat over coffee and gradually became reacquainted with reality. We had behaved like idiots. This was just the sort of seamanship which usually leaves us shaking our heads like a couple of buffers on The Squadron terrace. Whatever had got into us all of a sudden?

The answer, of course, was that this was a long weekend in early May – a few stolen days filled with the urgency that comes from much anticipation and a wine cellar depleted after a succession of long winter evenings spent poring over the pilot book.

In short, we were still operating on Shore Time.

It wasn't until much later that I realised the full significance of this. By then, it was August, and we had been sitting in Falmouth with all those other people who kept saying they were trying to get to the Scillies. We decided to move over to Helford for a couple of days to see if the rain looked any different from there.

We had played a certain amount of Scrabble, managed a good deal of laundry, the leak in the ventilator was fixed, and a temporary break in the clouds suggested a swift shopping expedition.

So how about being really adventurous? How about getting the bread at Helford Passage, on the other side of the river, for a change?

The book said there was a shop. The barmaid in the pub said it was three-quarters of a mile away.

And we townies, for whom shopping is a drive to Sainsbury's, set off for the two-mile hike down the lanes because – this being Cornwall – that's how far it turned out to be in the end.

But down these country lanes, there were butterflies in the deceptive Cornish hedges and clusters of buddleia poking over the cottage walls and a man and his dog to wish good morning and the time of day to be passed in the village stores when we finally reached them.

And, as we set off to walk the two miles back again, clutching the one small granary loaf like a trophy, it occurred to us that we were back in Boat Time - the kind that comes in limitless quantities and will carry you along as effortlessly as the tides.

If only you will let it.

The Good Stuff – Book One

Chapter 21
Beware the Singlehander

He had an original black Redstart with a puddle in the bottom. There was a French loaf balanced across his lap, and he rowed with that studied and leisurely pace which comes from not having to be anywhere particular in a hurry.

In short, he was a picture of the seasoned single-hander – a man at peace with himself and his world – and it was impossible not to smile and wish him good morning.

And therein lay the problem. As he paused and leaned on his oars, he drifted closer. By the time he had answered the polite questions about the whereabouts of the baker, he had his hand on the gunwale and was offering advice on the best places to anchor. Somehow it would have seemed rude not to invite him aboard for a coffee.

Coffee and a discussion of the local customs formalities led naturally to lunch and memories of cruises in years gone by. He sat there, expanding on his theme – indeed, expanding from one theme to another, as the talk moved imperceptibly from conversation to lecture.

The tide turned, the sun wandered off to the horizon, the hours drifted past and a wild panic began to set in among the crew that the old boy would never leave – that he would still be sitting there when the holiday ran out, holding up his mug for a refill and saying: "I remember one occasion when..."

And that, as my father would have said, is what you get for befriending a single-hander. As children, we were discouraged from talking to them – not particularly because anyone thought they would carry us off, but because, once adopted, they tended to move in and take over, like cuckoos.

It was not their fault, the parents explained. They were probably very nice chaps. It was just that they didn't often get the chance to talk.

It took me another 20 years to discover the truth of this. The occasion was my first long singlehanded voyage. What started out as an everyday cross-Channel trip became rather more serious somewhere off L'Aberwrac'h with the visibility down to a couple of hundred yards and a freighter charging out of the murk at 12 knots. I was so frightened, I turned left and didn't stop until I reached Guernsey.

This was a long way, and there was no one else to stand a watch. Nor was there anyone else to clean the fuel pump filter when it clogged or look up the frequency for La Corbière radio beacon when the boat lurched and jogged the dial - or, come to that, make coffee or read the log.

The trip ended up in something of a haze of exhaustion. When I arrived in St Peter Port, I slept for 20 hours – but I awoke with a sense of achievement that filled the cabin. In fact, the euphoria was too big for the cabin. I had to take it outside. I went for a walk on the pontoon.

The man on the boat opposite nodded Good Afternoon. He said he'd seen me come in. He asked if I'd come far. So I told him.

I told him about the crossing from Falmouth and the fog off the French coast and the freighter and the fuel filter. I may have missed out the coffee, but I'm sure I mentioned the RDF frequency because he had a funny glazed look on his face and muttered something about having to be getting along – so I changed the subject and told him about the log instead.

Of course, after he escaped and I came to my senses, I nearly died of embarrassment. Indeed, ever since then, I like to think of myself as positively reticent when it comes to more than the briefest greeting.

Except, of course, on special occasions - like, for instance, getting into Falmouth after what may still stand as the slowest ever passage from the Azores.

After making good only 11 miles in one 24-hour period, I began broadcasting "Is anyone there?" messages on the VHF. Eventually, I arrived after 17 days in company with a Dutchman, also singlehanded – but he had failed to reach the islands at all. After a fortnight, he ran out of holiday and had to turn back. He hadn't spoken to anyone for a month.

Over the whisky bottle in his cabin, he corrected this. He told me all about his trip – complete with readings from his log and a somewhat tortured translation of the poem he had written.

And then I told him about the joys of leaning over the rail and dropping torch batteries into the water and watching them go down and down, twinkling as they caught the light.

We were still talking when the sun came up.

Chapter 22
Doggone!

The dinghy was a long way down, and it was moving. The dog poked his nose over the rail and considered the prospect of jumping into it.

Slowly his tail sank to the deck. Surreptitiously, it crept between his legs. It re-emerged somewhere in the vicinity of his chin - and we realised we had a problem.

We wanted him to take to sailing. After all, a dog is not just for Christmas, a dog is also for those afternoons when you pick up the mooring in Langstone harbour and the tiresome business of taking him ashore can be transformed into a brisk and satisfying walk along the beach to the pub – if only the wretched animal will stop quivering on the rail and jump…

I stood in the dinghy, holding onto the guardrails and explained all this. Blue looked back at me with an expression which came straight off the RSPCA poster.

This was absurd. We'd been through all this. He had been introduced to boats in the most humane and gradual stages. We started out by wrapping him in a towel and hauling him aboard like freighted livestock. We bought him a smart new lifejacket with a handle on the top – and promptly made the obvious discovery that since the strap passes straight across his bladder, there are times when it is a very bad idea indeed.

Patiently, we taught him about the principles of tacking and how to keep his tail off the mainsheet track – about what happens when he puts all four feet into the coils of a genoa sheet. We even explained the futility of trying to dig his claws into a heeling glassfibre deck.

You would think that he could manage a little thing like jumping into a dinghy...

In the end, of course, he did. With a certain amount of pushing from one end and pulling from the other – not to mention enough platitudes to anaesthetise a pit bull terrier, he flopped into my arms, and a good deal of Langston harbour slopped over the side.

By the time we were all aboard, and the outboard fired up, the dog was doing his Bambi impression – eyes like saucers and legs at 45°. He stayed like that until the bow touched bottom, and he leapt over the side, hitting the beach like the Royal Marines.

So, anybody who might have witnessed all this - and wondered whether they ought to make a report to the relevant authority – would have been very surprised to note the difference on the return trip.

In the intervening couple of hours, the somewhat straightforward thought processes which go to make up what passes in Blue for intellect, had decided to associate the dinghy with the walk.

And this had been no ordinary walk. I don't know whether Southampton University's Department of Marine Biology has ever conducted any research into the death rate among fish in the eastern Solent, but it seemed that on this day most of them had taken themselves up onto the beach and were conducting some sort of competition to see who could decompose the fastest – and smell the most revolting.

Blue was in Heaven. He sniffed, he licked, he challenged his digestive tract with micro-organisms as yet undiscovered by veterinary science. He returned with his tail up, his tongue out and covered in sand. Then he leapt into the dinghy, filling that with sand as well and stood there as if to say: "OK, where next?"

Well, actually, it was round to the Hamble to show some prospective buyers over the boat. We still had the dinghy tied astern, and Blue, on his rounds, saw the way it rested conveniently against the pontoon. His brain filled once again with images of putrefying fish. He leapt aboard.

Inevitably, the basic principles of physics came into play: the kinetic energy generated by one leaping dog was transformed instantly into sideways drift.

It took a moment or two for him to realise it, but like Piglet in *Winnie the Pooh*, Blue was startled to find himself entirely surrounded by water.

People on adjoining boats began to point. A couple wheeling a trolley paused to await the outcome.

But the dog who, only 24 hours earlier, had to be levered ignominiously over the side, stood there and waved his tail while he drifted almost imperceptibly back again.

And when he jumped back onto the pontoon, it was with that studied nonchalance which comes to anyone contemplating a first single-handed voyage.

Now, if only he can only learn to row and tie a decent bowline…

———

Chapter 23
Sorry, Officer, I'm Sinking

The boat was full of water. It was sloshing around all over the cabin sole and washing in and out of the lockers under the bunks, turning the clothes into salty lumps and filling the wellies. Or, to put it another way, the boat was sinking.

You never forget the first time you find your boat sinking. Terror grips at your vitals, your eyes stare, your pulse races, you think of a dozen different things to do, none of them very sensible.

Abandon ship? Set off a flare? Start pumping?

The first time it happened to me, I got as far as the dinghy lashings before I thought to wonder just why the boat might be sinking. As usual, there was a perfectly simple explanation. She was a Caprice – an 18-footer of such minuscule displacement that with two people aboard, the cockpit drains drained in instead of out.

It was not something that had troubled me greatly until then – the extra weight never raised the waterline by more than half an inch, and so wet feet were about as close as we got to an emergency.

At least, they were until I removed the cockpit floor in a hurry and decided that resealing it could wait. Now, instead of wet feet, we had a boat full of water. When the panic subsided, I saved the ship with a couple of corks in the drains – I had corks instead of seacocks in those days. After that, all we needed to do was alter course for the nearest launderette.

Since then, I have found myself sinking on several occasions. There was the time, bringing *Largo* back from northern Spain single-handed in a north-easterly when it became abundantly clear that every time I put her on port tack, I had to pump every hour to stop the water slopping all over my feet as I sat at the chart table. The odd thing was that, on starboard, she was fine.

After a couple of days of this, when it seemed inevitable that we would end up in Greeland instead, ringing the office from Uummannaq and explaining: "I had no choice – the boat was sinking."

However, I remembered what happened when I called in to say I was fogbound in Alderney, and even the planes weren't running. It seemed a better idea to find the leak.

Over the next 24 hours, I wore out a perfectly good set of torch batteries looking in dark places for trickles of water. I crawled into the back of the engine to inspect the stern gland (such fun trying to crawl out again).

But all that happened was that the leak got worse. In fact, it went on getting worse whenever we were on port tack – and it did this for five years before I discovered a hairline crack in the scupper drain.

In five years, you get an awful lot of wet socks. There were times when I declared that the only thing that is necessary for supreme contentment in this life is the certain knowledge of precisely where your boat is leaking.

This winter, I revised that philosophy. A hard frost had been forecast and, dutifully, I drained the cooling water from the engine. I got the big socket wrench on the plug and then pottered about while the block started to empty itself slowly into the bilge.

By the time I had done a bit of packing and shut the forehatch and turned off the gas, water was still dribbling out. It always did take forever. I left it dribbling and went to make a phone call.

I came back. It was still dribbling.

This was ridiculous. I was going to be late. I didn't have time to hang about waiting for the last drop. Instead, I pumped the bilge, shut the hatch and left the water to look after itself.

But it did seem odd that it should have taken so long.

Maybe it was the traffic on the Winchester by-pass that provided the opportunity to ponder the question – or maybe it was the weariness that comes with two doses of the M3 in a single day – but the thought kept coming back: If the water was still running out after half an hour, how much more was there to come?

The answer dawned just short of the Basingstoke turn off: The answer was that there was the entire River Hamble still to come – if the seacock was open, that is…

I turned round in a hurry and headed back at speeds which might possibly have drawn the attention of the Hampshire Constabulary.

But I had my excuse all ready: "I had no choice, officer. The boat was sinking."

Chapter 24
Is There Anybody There?

Somebody whistled.

It was the sort of whistle you hear from the quay when you have your head in the engine – the sort you get from a fisherman who had decided he wants to reverse all over your warps.

Short and confident, it was a note not to be ignored.

Which was all very well except that it came 600 miles out in the Atlantic, and I was quite sure there was no one there to do any whistling.

I was single-handed – I was sure I was. In the week out from Falmouth, nobody had come stumbling down into the cabin to drip all over me and say: "Your watch, old man."

Nobody had crept sheepishly out of the hanging locker, saying: "I know this is a terrible inconvenience, but the police were after me…"

No pathetically grateful survivor had been pulled from a sinking liferaft – and now threatened to hog all the digestive biscuits for the remainder of the voyage. In short, I was alone and if someone was whistling, they had to be doing it from outside the boat.

With this certain knowledge, I leapt confidently into the companionway to greet the yacht I fully expected to see bobbing along within beer can-tossing range. There would be a cheery Frenchman at the wheel (nobody can be as laconic as the French when they try). We could hold a mid-ocean party, I thought, as I searched the immediate patch of water.

Nothing. Nothing that is, except for another, rather more insistent whistle.

This was beginning to get unnerving. At the time, I had only limited experience of hallucinations. Once, under conditions of heroic lack of sleep, I had felt the tremendously strong sensation that I Was Not Alone.

At the time, I was rather proud of this - almost as if I felt myself in the company of Joshua Slocum and his ghostly pilot of the *Pinta* (although, for him, the vision had been brought on by an overdose of goat's cheese and plums. I had overdosed on peanut butter and honey sandwiches).

Still, I tried to see it as an encouraging step forward in my paranormal development, ready for the time, years later, when I would make the mistake of hanging up my oilskins to dry – and then get the fright of my life when turning round and coming face to face with them, swaying gently under the forehatch and looking exactly like a hanged man.

But in the meantime, the phantom whistler was becoming impatient, and I was still groping for a logical explanation. I went back below, with some notion that it might be something to do with dolphins and sound waves coming through the hull.

In fact, it was nothing of the kind. It came screeching out of the VHF speaker – the VHF which was still switched to receive and which, after the Solent, I could no longer imagine being able to produce anything on channel 16 but endless chatter and calls for radio checks.

Tentatively, I picked up the microphone and whistled back. Immediately, a conversational voice broke in.

"Hello sailboat, where are you bound for?"

Who was this? Was it some kind of Universal Presence checking up on me? I was too startled to say anything, which meant the voice went on: "I'm bound for Charlestown, in ballast."

Ah! Now we were getting somewhere. I was almost certain that Supreme Beings never went anywhere in ballast - and certainly not to Charlestown. I took another look out of the hatch.

And there, steaming across *Largo's* bows at a range of about a mile, was a huge, rusty freighter. I was rather startled to find him there - after all, had I not just looked? How could something that big get that close without my knowing?

What had happened, of course, was that I had become so used to being a solitary yacht on a limitless ocean that I had stopped looking.

Oh, I was fine at night: I set the alarm for 20-minute intervals, and each time it rang, I leapt out of bed to scan the horizon for supertankers. The fact that I hardly ever saw one was beside the point.

But by daylight, in perfect visibility, I just assumed that if something was there, I would see it.

After all, when you're coastal cruising at home, you don't make a point of regular all-round checks and setting alarms to make sure you don't miss one. There's always so much traffic about that watch-keeping comes naturally.

And, just as naturally, when there's nothing around, your world contracts. Mine, in this instance, had contracted to a space 32ft long and 9ft 8in wide.

Which is really rather absurd when you consider that the whole point of ocean cruising is to broaden your horizons.

Chapter 25
Two's Company

After a while, the singlehanded racing yachtsman gets a bit of a reputation. It's all to do with having a number painted on the hull and an Aries hanging off the stern; people think the skipper must be something of a hero.

This never worried me greatly. I might not be a Chichester or a Knox-Johnston but I can wax fairly lyrical on the subject of sleep deprivation off the Grand Banks or clocking 1,200 miles in nine days to come second in class in the Azores and Back (I have the engraved decanter to prove it).

But when someone looked down from the quay in Weymouth last summer, took in the name on the stern and shouted: "Oi, aren't you supposed to be singlehanded?" it seemed that things had gone too far.

Tamsin was understandably miffed. She was, at the time, engaged in her role as one of the local sights – perched in the cockpit and plying the handle of our patent manual washing machine – a device which would not look out of place in an agricultural museum. But then she had never understood the attractions of singlehanded sailing, not least when I tried to explain the delights of being able to take meals straight from the saucepan without anyone complaining.

Of course, there is more to it than that. Certainly, there are moments when sailing alone over long distances can elevate a certain type of person to some sort of cosmic state of supreme contentment. Even pop stars, with all their pharmaceuticals, rarely manage this. But, at the same time, it does have its drawbacks.

I well remember my first long solo trip, from Poole to Northern Spain: by the time I got there, I was so bursting with pride, I could hardly wait to tell someone – anyone. In the end, I was reduced to going ashore for a solitary dinner and hoping for a chatty waitress (I didn't get one). But that is now part of a different and former existence. Now is the time to celebrate the pleasures of not being singlehanded. These, I should add, do not include sharing your life with a row of gorillas, whose idea of companionship is four hours jammed together on the weather rail and who learned their personal hygiene in the rugby club changing room. Nor do I suggest getting up in the middle of the night to join one of those floating cocktail parties – the ones which move from marina to marina and measure the success of the cruise by the volume of laughter in the cockpit at 0100.

No, this is about the backbone of the sailing fraternity: The cruising couple.

It would be unworthy, somehow, to start without recalling the magnificent teamwork involved in extracting the conduit from Largo's mast without breaking it, demolishing anything particularly expensive or ending up on the sofa at Relate. Similarly, I see nothing sexist in appreciating the company of someone who can distinguish the leading marks as dusk falls on one of those tortuous Brittany rivers – and then asks brightly: "All right if I go and cook now?"

As a couple, you can invite the people on the next boat over for a drink and find that they don't hesitate, thinking that maybe you haven't spoken to a soul since Dover and intend to pin them behind one warm beer for the rest of the day, lecturing them into a state of coma.

And, come the evening, the pair of you can sit in the cockpit in companionable silence and watch the comings and goings in the anchorage.

"Comings and goings", of course, means fully-crewed yachts going round and round with everybody gesticulating before picking exactly the wrong spot.

Seasoned couples do not do things like that. It's the newbies who make the evening echo to a duet of

"Darling, for God's sake, get it round something…"

"Darling, I'm trying to. If only you wouldn't go so fast, Darling."

Instead, the theory is that the sailing couple develops a rapport which has as much to do with togetherness as boat handling and which means that, but for the occasional discreet gesture, the manoeuvre is performed ostensibly by telepathy. And then, when all is secure, and the first noisy party from the next trot sets off for the pub, they can wrap a bottle of wine in a wet towel, climb into the dinghy and drift very gently up the river on the tide.

The first time we did this was on the Beaulieu River in Hampshire. We went so slowly that the ducks overtook us. When, finally, we rounded the bend into that hidden pool intended for bilge-keelers and poets, we found an elderly Westerly anchored there with a solitary figure in the cockpit, glass in hand, face tilted to the evening sun. He opened his eyes, looked over the side and, in a conversational tone which carried in the stillness, remarked: "You look happy."

And he was right.

Chapter 26
One Careful Owner

The buyer stood in the cabin and made his offer. He made it hurriedly and rather loudly because, just at that moment, the prospective buyer started banging on the hull with his fist.

Anyone who ever tried to sell a boat should experience something like this once in their lives; it feels wonderful. The only trouble is that it does lead to a certain amount of embarrassment. My problem was that, just as I accepted the offer, the prospective buyer started climbing the ladder: The three of us ended up in the cockpit simultaneously, and I had to do the explaining.

There are people, I suppose (the sort of people who buy and sell boats with the regularity of sock-changing) who find all this perfectly normal. But for those of us who view the sale of a well-loved yacht after 12 years to be an event comparable with divorce, the whole business becomes rather unsettling.

The fact that the buyer turned out not to be a buyer at all but merely someone who was rather too enthusiastic only added to the sense of desperation – particularly when I drove a long way to collect a cheque for the deposit and he explained that he didn't actually have the money – not as such, not at the moment and, well, he wasn't entirely sure when he would have the money.

But by this stage, I had begun to realise that everything to do with selling boats takes place in a parallel universe – one where time is cyclical, and nothing ever reaches a conclusion.

It is also a universe peopled by some real collector's items. Take, for instance, the man who wanted a boat to die on…

Yes, I thought it was odd. But he was perfectly serious. He was very ill, he explained, and would never be cured because he would never again let a doctor near him. This was not unreasonable considering his experiences in the surgery: his last doctor had told him that unless he gave up sailing, he would be dead within a year. He did give up sailing and promptly became so miserable that his wife left him. This, of course, made him even more depressed. By the time he came to see *Largo,* he was in a state of terminal decline and clearly relishing every moment. "She'll make a good coffin," he said, wandering around shaking the rigging. When we set off for a trial sail, the feel of a tiller under his hand transformed his expression to one of supreme contentment – rather as if he was ready for the angels at that precise moment.

It was just as well that his offer was based on a calculation which seemed to involve his life expectancy. I had no qualms about refusing him. Apart from anything else, I couldn't condemn *Largo* to a lingering death as well. We took a trip down to the West Country with a "For Sale" sign hanging in the rigging but found that it only turned us into a miniature Boat Show. People who walk around marinas the same way they walk around SeaWorld came and knocked and looked and said: "How far can you go in it?"

We were happier with the market trader who raised the business of bargaining to the level of an art form. First, he arrived on the pontoon and blocked out the light: he was a very large man indeed. Then he stepped on the side deck, and *Largo* - no lightweight herself - promptly heeled to 20°. He took a look; he rattled the rigging, he offered to write a cheque.

What, no survey? Not even: "I have a friend who knows about boats. Would it be alright if he came and had a look?"

No, "I'll have to think about it and call you on Monday." Instead, just a hand in the back pocket and a confident stare.

It was all a bit unnerving: I mean, what do you do? You have to take him seriously. We got to withing £500 of each other which, on a £20,000 boat, is the price of pride.

He went and sat in his car and waited patiently. We sat in the cockpit and worried furiously. I went ashore and made an ostentatious phone call. He went on sitting in his car, watching. It was like playing chess with Kasparov, only bigger.

In the end, *Largo* went to the couple who sat in the cabin and drank beer, looked at the pictures on the bulkhead, listened to the stories and grinned at each other in that way which comes to those who know they have simultaneously made an important discovery.

Tamsin said that out of all the dozens who had come and looked and poked and rattled over eight months, these were the ones, and as usual in such matters, she was right.

So if you find yourself snug against the quay one day and a somewhat anxious young couple in a Rival 32 come ranging up alongside, please take their lines and give them a smile. *Largo* has a new life.

That was Clare and Peter Davies. I had forgotten their names until I wrote a blog post bemoaning what seemed to be the lack of dolphins on the first trip to the Azores with Samsara. Peter wrote to me, saying there were still plenty around Falmouth and The Scillies – and if I wanted to come and meet them, why didn't I come and see my old boat while I was at it?

Can you believe it? She was still in the same ownership 25 years later.

Eventually, we met off St Just. They came and tied up alongside, and we had a beer together (socially distanced in those days). I crawled all over my old boat, marvelling that the locker that was only good for keeping burgee sticks was still there. She still had the same mainsheet, for heaven's sake … and the winch under the boom for my Heath Robinson reefing system ("What's wrong with it," said Peter. "It works fine.")

Mind you; he had replaced the electrics. I can't blame him.

They have no plans to look for another boat – why would they?

———

Chapter 27
Beyond the Pale

Look, this is embarrassing. I've bought a catamaran.

There, it's out – and I feel rather as if I have admitted to eating peas with my knife.

Of course, it's all to do with conditioning. I grew up sailing a Folkboat out of Walton Backwaters. We used to look down on Stellas because they had an extra plank and another three inches headroom. "Caravans", we used to call them.

As for catamarans, well they were completely beyond the pale. They looked like blocks of flats or giant insects. According to Father, catamarans either turned over or broke up. If they were not sailed by crazed young men who kept being rescued, saying: "I'll get it right next time. I know where I've gone wrong, now...", then it was over-anxious couples – she in pink slacks and he in a white-topped yachting cap with an anchor on the front.

And now, eight months after setting foot on a cruising cat for the first time, I have one of my own. She is a Heavenly Twins. She is 27ft overall and 13ft 9in in the beam. She looks like a funny little duck sitting on the water, and we are calling her *Lottie Warren* after my great-grandfather's ship. He'd turn in his grave if he knew.

Just how all of this came about so suddenly has my head spinning. A week before, looking for the first time into a catamaran cabin – and picking our jaws off the floor and our eyebrows off the deckhead, we had our hearts set on a 40ft steel cutter (steel for safety and 40ft to live aboard). When we found that the only one we could afford sailed like a bucket, we went to the Southampton Boat Show in a state of some despondency.

And that was where we met our friendly Devil's Advocate: "Why don't you look at a catamaran. They don't sink, and they've bags of room."

So, over the winter, we drove hundreds of miles looking at catamarans. We even drove to Lorient (the bootful of wine had nothing to do with it).

Worst of all, we devoured books on catamarans. Every one of

them was written by an enthusiast, gripped with a fervour that would do justice to one of those people who come to the door with pamphlets about the Day of Judgement.

In this case, the irrefutable tracts began with: "For thousands of years, the multihull has been the vessel of choice for transporting people – and it still is."

Then there was the photocopied magazine article by the man who went round the world singlehanded in a Heavenly Twins and was hit by "an absolute monster of a freak wave". He came through unscathed, the little boat surfing sideways with the breaking crest. The treacle fell off the table, though.

Pretty soon, I found myself doodling with lists of comparative advantages and disadvantages: Did being able to run before the trades at ten knots without rolling the gunwales under outweigh the lesser windward performance in heavy weather? Was the problem of being wind-rode in a crowded anchorage really so bad if you could sit on the beach instead?

And then there was the test sail – 13knots reaching into Chichester Harbour. The most I ever got out of my Rival was 9.7, and that was with everything straining in a gale, and lasted just long enough for the log to record it as a new top speed before we were hurled into a broach which left us dead in the water with everything flapping.

But the little cat surfed on and on. I couldn't believe it. Nor, come to that, could the broker – although, of course, he made a reasonable stab at taking it in his stride.

All this helped a bit, but there was still the problem of the pink slacks and the assumption that the real reason people buy catamarans is because they don't like all that "keeling over" and the china horses falling off the windowsill.

So we went to the Owners Association Annual Dinner and Dance. This was another eye-opener. I had hoped that our fellow-members would be impressed with our ambitious cruising plans. Not a bit of it. They all had plans of their own which involved a lot more mileage – and certainly more sunshine.

And when the main prize was awarded to a couple who had

circumnavigated and accepted on their behalf by another couple who had just spent three years in the Med, I became rather subdued. Every time we changed places (the men shifted two places to the left after each course), people asked: "And when were you converted?"

It seems that multihull sailors spend so much time justifying their boats to sceptical – not to say – derisive monohull owners that they develop something of a siege mentality.

Not that I have, of course. Dogwatch is nothing if not a balanced view of the sailing scene.

But if you see a funny-looking little cat doing 13 knots up the river, please be good enough to get out of the way.

Chapter 28
Tackling Everest

The dog stood on the deck and looked at the quay. This being Rye at low tide, it meant pointing his nose high in the air - something which tends to make him look pathetically appealing at the best of times.

To this, he added an expression of intense concern as he measured the vertical distance between himself and the start of his walk.

We had known that one day it would come to this. We had taught him to climb on and off pontoons, in and out of dinghies, up and down companionways, but never before had he come up against 12 feet of ladder.

For a time, I had entertained the vague hope that he would prove to be one of those remarkable dogs who learn to climb ladders. I made a big production out of telling him about the Labrador who could do it. But Blue just looked at me as if I was mad and continued to stare at the edge of Strand Quay – or, as it had now become, his personal Everest.

Of course, there were alternatives: we could dress him up in his lifejacket and hoist him up by the handle on his back – but this might well have some unfortunate consequences. We knew all about the strap that passed directly over his bladder. Besides, the walk was becoming more overdue by the minute.

We could put him in a rucksack. The idea possessed a certain charm and would make for some wonderful photographs, but the only time we tried it, the effect was rather like stuffing an octopus into a carrier bag.

So we were left face to face with the inevitable. Blue would have to be carried up the ladder.

Considering his size and his bad breath, he does not get picked up very often, so he leapt into my arms with a good deal of enthusiasm.

It lasted just long enough to begin the crossing from the boat to the ladder – along three feet of single rope footbridge swaying like the one in the Indiana Jones films. (I had just made the discovery that, when drying out in a catamaran, you keep the warps taught, or you end up yards away from the quay).

Actually, I don't think it was the possibility of falling in the mud that upset Blue. Indeed, in the early stages, in between lunching off my ear, I suspect he was confiding: "Hey, I can walk through this stuff, no trouble."

But when we got halfway up and looked down, he lost his nerve.

With hindsight, it would have been better if the moment had not coincided with the discovery that my one free hand was now gripping a rung somewhere down by my knees. If we were going to make any more progress, this hand would have to be moved - something that would not be terribly easy, given that the other one was full of dog.

Meanwhile, the dog chose this moment to decide that he did want to learn to climb ladders after all - and appeared to have grown half a dozen extra legs for the purpose.

Tamsin looked down from the top and said: "Are you all right?"

Now, I never like to say, "No" to a question like that. When I admit defeat, I like to qualify things a bit. However, there really was very little to bolster the confidence. In the end, I said: "Er, I don't think this is going to work."

It ought to have worked: Had I not carried enough shopping up and down ladders over the years? I was something of an expert in the art of climbing ladders one-handed.

All the same, I had to admit that I had not carried my Tescos bags clasped to my chest with two feet of French bread resting on my shoulder and a damp nose of liver sausage nuzzling my ear. For one thing, the centre of gravity would be all wrong.

There was only one thing for it. Very gently, I extracted a finger from somewhere underneath the dog and felt for the ladder.

Very quietly, I began a hypnotic chant: "Good dog. There's a good dog. What a good dog…"

The wriggling stopped. So did the breathing.

And the next few seconds did not, after all, find us falling headfirst into the mud in a tangle of fur and recriminations.

Instead, we skipped up the last few rungs with a flourish, and Blue trotted off across the grass as if there had been no more to it than sniffing at the back door until someone let him out.

It had all turned out to be so unexpectedly easy that I almost looked forward to the return journey when a happily exhausted hound would nestle once again in my arms, and the audience of passers-by would be impressed all over again.

I was almost right. The only difference was that, after the walk, the armful consisted of one part dog to five parts mud. By the time we reached the deck, I might just as well have fallen in headfirst.

Chapter 29
Marked for Life

The plastic pot marked "Shackles" does indeed contain shackles. The batteries (large) are similarly at home, and "Glues 1" nestles next to "Glues 2" as neatly as the spice racks in Delia Smith's kitchen.

From time to time, visitors profess themselves astonished that for one so confused by life ashore, I manage to run such a well-ordered ship.

It is, of course, nothing to do with me. For years I knew where the shackles were kept because I knew where they had always been kept. The charts were catalogued according to a system more historical than geographical, and I don't suppose there was a label on anything at all in the spares locker.

But then came the day I had to turn *Largo* over to a delivery crew. Frankly, I would rather have sailed her back across the Atlantic myself. At one point, I began experimenting with calculations for crossing the finishing line and heading straight back to Plymouth.

But the arrangements were made. I had to go back to work, and my friends Janet and John were devoting their summer holiday to the business of getting the boat home without me.

They arrived in Newport while I was up the mast. This was not intentional, but it did mean I could descend triumphantly, bringing with me the masthead spinnaker fitting – now worn to the dimension of my grandmother's wedding ring. It had taken a lot of spinnaker work to do that, I pointed out. I could tell they were impressed.

They were, however, not impressed when they went below. The thing about Janet and John is that they are Yachtmasters. John is even an instructor. He skippers sail training vessels. For a holiday cruise, they head for somewhere like Spitzbergen. They do not put to sea in anything but a thoroughly seamanlike manner.

During the ensuing two days, John gave the boat a complete survey – short of physically taking her out of the water. He took a screwdriver to all the seacocks, a spanner to the rigging – he even found his way with a handful of tools into the back of the engine whence no one has ever returned with all their skin.

But by the time I set off for Boston airport with a quite astonishing amount of luggage, he pronounced himself satisfied and promised to deliver the boat back to the Hamble by mid-September.

It was the longest summer I can remember. I had never let anybody sail *Largo* before. Would they remember to turn off the seacock in the head? Had I told them how the emergency steering fitted together? Would they drop the sextant? (I nearly did).

When a postcard arrived from the Azores, I felt like Mrs James Cook, getting the news about the friendly inhabitants of Tahiti. I scanned the cheery message for meaning between the lines: "Third in the OCC pursuit race." I hoped they hadn't been pushing her.

Then there was: "Only took the umbrella down for the evening sight." A café umbrella, this, with the sponsor's name on the top and a nasty sharp point on the bottom. How had they fixed it? What was it doing to the gelcoat?

By the time they arrived back on the Hamble, I no longer imagined the worst. I was convinced of it.

Of course, I never admitted to any of this. I just sat in the cockpit nodding and smiling – and taking surreptitious glances at the gear.

It had been perfectly straightforward, they told me. Everything was fine, and the boat behaved perfectly.

But was that really what they were thinking? Was there not something else on their minds - like, for instance, the reason why every single rope which had previously ended in a piece of sticky plastic tape was now neatly whipped? There was even whipping on the chafed patch halfway along the genoa sheet – and it had been like that ever since I'd had the boat.

In the head, there was a smartly printed reminder "Close Seacock"; in the same hand, on every pot and container down to the last, most insignificant plastic bag, a clearly labelled list of contents.

But they never mentioned the hours they must have spent working their way through the boat with a felt-tipped pen – including the pot which now so ostentatiously contained "Sailmaking (misc)".

For a long time, in an absurd way, I resented it. Everything was still in the place I had chosen for it. I could put my hand on the shackles with my eyes shut in the middle of a moonless night. But seeing the pot with its neat and pedantic label only reminded me of the time *Largo* had crossed an ocean without me.

Not anymore, of course. Now *Largo* has gone to a new home – without the pots…

Now they are in their new stowage aboard *Lottie Warren* – and without Janet's labels, I wouldn't have a clue what is in them.

Chapter 30
Holland Revisited

There is no nostalgia like the nostalgia for boats. For me, it begins in the 1960s – the days when the old Ferrograph depth recorder was considered a fantastic invention, and nobody had thought of carrying a liferaft. If you sank, you climbed into your 6ft pram dinghy and fired off flares until that sank, too.

In those days, a 30footer was considered a big boat - although, of course, nobody called her a 30footer. She was a seven tonner just as depths were in fathoms and rigging in $^3/_{16}$ths or $^1/_4$in.

But lately, I have been preoccupied with memories that go back to the days before glass fibre and Kevlar and GPS. Last summer, I went back to the old cruising ground, retracing the route and finding that the old photographs in the family album came to life all over again. Suddenly the entries in the tattered logbook on the bottom shelf of my parents' bookcase acquired a substance far beyond its fading ink.

This time, the aim was no longer to venture just a bit further than the previous year. This time we were not merely going to discover new harbours and explore virgin pages of the pilot book. This time the search was for nostalgia. At times it seemed like a pilgrimage – a passage of 100 miles across the North Sea but 35 years back in time.

The first time I cruised the Dutch canals was in 1960. There were five of us in *Torgunn,* a Folkboat with no headroom and a Stuart Turner petrol engine with no neutral and certainly no reverse.

It was the memory of advancing on bridges at a steady three knots with absolutely no possibility of stopping that made me appreciate the modern conveniences of the 90s. *Lottie Warren*, a 27ft Heavenly Twins catamaran, may not be exactly overpowered with her 9.9hp Yamaha outboard - but you can slam it in reverse, and the big, three-bladed prop will stop you in a couple of lengths.

Back in 1960, all we could do was develop a technique which we called "bridgemanship" and which owed something to the game of chicken as played by American teenagers living near freeways. We would give three blasts on our puny, brass, mouth-operated foghorn and advance boldly with all the confidence of a ship's company who knew they had right on their side.

The bridge-keeper, who may have been trying to clear a traffic jam or waiting for enough boats to make opening the bridge worthwhile, would look down from his control box at the tiny English yacht and assume that at any moment, Father would yank the gear lever backwards.

There was, of course, no gear lever. There was just Father with his jaw set in that peculiar manner that suited Jack Hawkins so well in *The Cruel Sea*, and Mother, with her knuckles glowing white – and my sisters and I jumping up and down with excitement, as we waited to see who would back down first.

Invariably it was the bridge-keeper. By the time he realised what was about to happen, we were close enough to see the expression on his face as he grabbed for his machinery. The bridge swung away just as *Torgunn's* forestay was about the pluck the pigeons off the parapet.

On other occasions father would growl: "Going round!" and thrust the tiller across the cockpit, sweeping one or more of his children with it. The boat would heel to 30° as we screamed into an about-turn which really should not have been possible for a long-keeled design like a Folkboat.

This time the only comparable occasion was when *Lottie Warren* was the last boat entering the massive *Volkeraksluizen* just south of Willemstadt. When we were still 50 yards from the entrance, the lock-keeper suddenly turned his traffic lights from green to red and started closing the gates.

Lottie Warren is 13ft 9n in the beam, and we suffer from that particular disorder common to most converts from monohulls: all gaps look small.

I shunted into reverse, and *Lottie* stopped dead. A moment later, there was an echoing metallic click, and from somewhere in the heavens, the bored voice of the bridge-keeper boomed: "OK, come on, then. But quickly, please."

Of course, the last time I was in Willemstadt, there was no lock. That was 1962 and our first season with *Bellrock of Mersea*, a 28ft Sterling – the forerunner of Kim Holman's Twister. We had made the move up when we realised that five people in a Folkboat was not really a recipe for domestic harmony – particularly with Father's habit of getting up in the night to check the warps.

Anyway, it was in Willemstadt with *Bellrock* that we found out why the Dutch built the *Volkeraksluizen* and all the other locks and dams of the Delta Project. Admittedly, what happened on August 6th, 1962, was a pale shadow of the terrible storm of January 31st 1953, when the dykes were breached in 89 places, and 1,853 people drowned.

But '62 was still an alarming experience. A westerly Force 9 pumped the high tide into the delta, piled it up into the harbour at Willemstadt and seriously threatened to float *Bellrock* down the main street.

We had half a dozen boats outside us, and the sound of groaning planking and straining frames is something that surfaces for me even now when bad dreams intrude on a night spent up against a harbour wall.

Still, two days later, the log records: "Wonderful beat to Veere in Force 5 with tide all the way."

Odd that, having a tide in what is now the *Verse Meere*. But then, so was the entry for Amsterdam: "Lousy yacht haven. Dirty and uncomfortable." That was the *Spoorhaven* which even today is described in the pilot book as "not recommended as it has no facilities and is exposed to constant road traffic noise and wash from barges."

As we passed by on our way to the new Sixhaven Marina, we could see what Mother meant. Every mast swung to and fro in its own agonising rhythm as the chop hurled itself through the open piling. It was there in 1960 that the herring disappeared down the back of the cooker, and we decided we preferred the alternative Dutch delicacy: *frites* in a paper cone with a large dollop of mayonnaise.

I am still rather partial to them – and in among the old photographs, I find one of me at the age of 13, sitting on the bank of a canal eating *frites* with my childhood sweetheart. We were sailing in company with her family in their ten-tonner, *Julia*. I remember *Julia* sailed like a bucket, which was why, a few years later, the sweetheart's brother and his friends wrecked her after failing to claw off a lee shore in Denmark.

The childhood sweetheart went off and married someone else, as they do, but Tamsin determined to buy the choicest and freshest produce in every market we passed.

Not that we did too badly in 1962. As the logbook records: "Lovely trip along the canal. Tied up in the centre of Haarlem for *fondue Bourgignon.*"

Nobody ties up the centre of Haarlem now. You end up in the marina a mile away to the north or in the suburbs to the south.

Actually, there are times when that is no bad thing – times like on the hour and the half-hour and, quite frequently, the quarter-hour. It was not something I remembered from the 1960s, but the Dutch are very keen on their Town Hall clocks - all of which have bells and possibly mechanical displays with marching figures going in and out of little doorways like cuckoos. In Middelburg, the peal lasted for a full two minutes and seemed to change with the hours. On one occasion, they played *Land of Hope and Glory.*

In Veere, they chimed on the half-hour because the clock has no minute hand. The peal was long and complicated, and we wondered whether there was something wrong with the mechanism because, wherever you expected the tune to go, it never seemed to arrive.

Still, we had the means to get away even if, in Veere we were moored practically in the belfry. This time we had bicycles: We bought them in the second-hand market in Amsterdam when we realised that in Holland, the highest form of life is the bicycle – above even the canal barge on the evolutionary scale and certainly on an entirely different ladder from the motor car.

They were fairly basic bicycles and, of course, they had those peculiar Continental brakes, but since Dutch bicycles do not have to stop for anything, maybe brakes are not so important.

Anyway, we travelled for miles on those bikes and, in between harbours, they stood proudly on the foredeck where, we liked to think, they gave us a certain amount of canal credibility.

The idea was that when we reached Vlissingen, we were going to sell them to an incoming crew, but the idea fell apart when the five weeks of uninterrupted sunshine came to an abrupt end, and we found ourselves waiting for three days for a vicious nor'easter to abate. In the end, we had to sail back across the North Sea with the bikes still parked on the foredeck.

But then, the return trip across the North Sea is invariably more complicated than the outward passage. Still, as the old logbook concludes: "Forecast at last good. Glorious reach through the moonlit night in Easterly 3-4. Brightlingsea for customs clearance, then home."

Thirty-three years on, a southerly filled in during the night, and *Lottie Warren* romped up to the Pye End buoy outside Walton Backwaters with the spinnaker pulling and nobody caring about formalities.

In another 30 years, I like to think we'll do it all again.

Reading this 27 years later; doesn't it make you just so angry that we in the UK could have been so gullible as to throw away our EU membership? So, the answer is, no, I couldn't just go and spend the summer in Holland again – not if I'd spent too long in France or Spain or Portugal or anywhere else that would add up to a total of more than 90 days in the EU. I'm sorry. It just makes me weep with frustration.

If you can bear it, I go on about this in the "Opinion" page of the blog – and on… and on…

Chapter 31
Space Craft

One of my earliest memories of sailing is a smell. It is pungent, sickly sweet and coming from the back of the cooker. It is the smell of decomposing herring. How the herring got down the back of the cooker is one of those old family legends which improves with the telling...

We were in Holland for the first time. We were in a Folkboat. We had never tasted the Dutch delicacy of raw herring and did not know that the wash from the big ships – in those days, at last – came straight through the wooden breakwater to set the yachts rolling their gunwales under.

Between these last two discoveries was a third: that none of us liked raw herring. It was just unfortunate that Mother began to fry it as the *SS Supertanker* went by.

Frying pan and contents disappeared down the back of the cooker, closely followed by the collective sense of humour. This was my first lesson in that essential truth about boats: every one of them has a space somewhere which nobody can reach.

Of course, I didn't begin to learn the lesson at that stage. First, I had to wait for the day I decided to instal an Autohelm in my own boat.

Given that *Amicus* was a Caprice and only 18ft overall (and I was convinced that the correct route for the wiring was via the lazarette), this was called learning the hard way.

I started by thinking I could work by feel: both hands in the locker, face pressed to the deck and that look of concentration on my face which normally goes with deep philosophical thought.

This was hopeless. For all I knew, I was going to drill through the bottom of the boat. I stuck my head down the hatch to see what was going on.

It followed that my shoulders had to go too – and then sometime later, in that compelling sort of sequence of events which causes most of the world's more spectacular disasters, various other parts of the body...

From the point of view of installing the Autohelm, this was certainly an improvement. Once I was ensconced inside the lazarette, able to see what I was doing, both hands on the drill, braced – well, squashed – against the stern, I could really get things done.

It was when I had finished getting things done that the trouble began. I couldn't get myself out.

No, that was not true. The very idea was absurd. It was surely only a matter of reversing the procedure for getting in - after all, what goes up must come down and all that.

Somewhere, a small voice countered with the old chestnut about toothpaste and getting it back into the tube. But this was not the same thing at all. If only I could get my left leg out from under my right leg and shift my shoulder so…

What I needed was some help. I toyed with the idea of calling for help. Then I wondered what anyone was supposed to do, in the unlikely event that there was someone out there to hear a muffled cry from any one of a number of apparently deserted boats.

I began to panic. That was it: I would panic, and with the superhuman strength that comes from adrenalin, I would kick my way out through the hull.

It would be interesting to know whether I would have gone ahead with this. In the event, it dawned on me just in time that if I did kick a hole in the hull, then the boat would instantly sink with me still stuck in the lazarette.

The fact that I am here to tell the tale means that I did, ultimately, get out of there: the boatyard foreman did not find me still trapped when he arrived to lift the mooring the following December - *"Yachtsman got stuck, coroner told."*

If I did not learn the lesson about small, inaccessible spaces on that occasion, then probably I never will. Certainly, the back of *Largo's* engine holds no fears for me. Happily, I will spend afternoons in the cockpit locker, an exercise which might readily be included in the handbook for the Boy Scout pot-holing badge.

So it came as no surprise that, when the time came to install a new water hose in *Lottie Warren's* bow locker – a space about the size of a dog kennel and devoted in equal parts to buoyancy, fresh water and the sort of rubbish that would normally belong in a garden shed – I disappeared headfirst through the hatch like a circus acrobat going through a hoop.

Only afterwards did I think about turning round. That is why the following day found me dismantling the hatch cover to straighten the hinges (the watertight seal had started to make a clicking noise, rather as if someone has sat on it).

But this sort of thing is just a part of the learning curve. I'll know better next time.

Chapter 32
It's a Seadog's Life

The dog has his own cabin.

Yes, ridiculous, isn't it? When we agreed that Blue was to say goodbye forever to the Lone Valley Dog Ranch and become a regular member of *Lottie Warren's* crew, we assumed he would be grateful. Certainly, he seemed pathetically pleased to be included on the occasional trip aboard our old boat *Largo,* the Rival 32.

During his first tentative introduction on the mooring, he had allowed himself to be swayed aboard wrapped in a towel like some sort of unaccompanied livestock for export.

When we took him out into the Solent for the first time, he soon added the command "Lee-oh!" to his 20-word vocabulary (along with walkies, lead, dog food, etc.)

And when he spent his first night aboard, sleeping in a banana box under the saloon table (lowered into its alternative function as a double berth) he never so much as uttered a whimper – no matter what went on an inch above his head.

In the morning, we just slid him out again as you would the bottom drawer, and he promptly came alive like something out of *The Nutcracker.* But now that he has spent a good part of the summer afloat and acquired the confidence of a regular boat dog, he has begun to make his own arrangements.

We noticed the subtle shift when he discovered the benefits of marina living. He stopped walking down the pontoons eyeing the water below and moving with the bow-legged gait of an arthritic tightrope walker. Now he preened and posed as people stopped and exclaimed: "Look, there's a dog in a lifejacket."

After a while, we began to tire of this - the Crewsaver was not supposed to be a fashion item. We just thought that if ever he were to fall in, the prospect of seeing a small black head in the water could only be matched by the difficulty in pulling him out again.

Actually, he has only fallen in once, and then it was in the marina. But if you have never seen a dog trying to climb four feet of vertical fibreglass, you have not witnessed real panic.

Most of the time, he treats life afloat rather as I imagine my grandfather must have treated his one week of the year chartering the old Xenia at Cowes in the 1920s. The sepia photographs show the old boy posing with his cronies by the wheel. They all wore identical reefer jackets, yachting caps and whites, and all appeared to be trying rather desperately to look as though they belonged.

Blue belongs. Every morning, he takes his constitutional on the foredeck, does his bending and stretching exercises and settles down to keep an eye on the world. From time to time, people come past and say: "Look, there's a dog in a lifejacket!" and he poses and looks haughty - but mostly it's a matter of checking out the smells borne on the wind: mud, rotting vegetation, raw sewage - all the good things in life.

When the time comes to get underway, he likes to stand up, hoist his tail in the wind and go down the river like a figurehead (oh, look, there's a figurehead in a lifejacket!" It's much the same coming into port at the end of the day.

It is just unfortunate that, between times, life afloat is interrupted by the open sea. The open sea is not something Blue cares for – not since a dollop of it joined him on the foredeck aboard Largo. When that happens, he comes back to the cockpit and sits wedged behind the helmsman's knees, looking pathetic.

Still, it's all forgotten at the end of the day when the time comes to go ashore. Then he stands in the bow of the dingy ready to leap for the jetty as soon as we get within ten yards – the fact that Blue can only leap two yards has yet to discourage him.

Coming back is more of a problem. This is because he is invariably covered in mud. We have tried to teach him to sit in the bow, but apparently, his vocabulary reached capacity with the addition of "Lee-oh", and he has to trample mud all over the rest of the dinghy first.

To begin with, I thought this was a good way of cleaning his feet - until he finished off the job by doing a couple of circuits of *Lottie's* decks as well. But, by this time, just as we wondered whether a dog on a boat was such a good idea, he would saunter off to his cabin – with his own 6ft 6in x 3ft berth, his own red-and-yellow striped duvet (which he would immediately kick aside, all the better to dry himself on the royal blue velour underneath).

And there he would stay until he heard the first stirrings from the next-door cabin in the morning.

It makes you wonder what they mean by "a dog's life."

———————

Chapter 33
Pan-Pan Medico

It is one of the Laws of Nature that toothache, like childbirth, much prefers the small hours. You can be brave about it – or at least you can be lazy, turn over and hope it will go away. But eventually, there is only one recourse. I stumbled out of bed in search of aspirin.

The medical kit lives in the locker under the sink. It consists of a pair of two-litre ice cream tubs, one inscribed with the word "Pills" and the other called "Dressings". Blinking under the glare of the fluorescent light, I ripped the top off "Pills" and started to rummage.

There were pills in there for seasickness, pills for inflammation of the muscles, little bottles of capsules for constipation and indigestion. There were ointments and potions and powders, and something called Dr Collis Brown's Pills, which are apparently very effective for digestive disorders and sounded as though they out to have come out of a patent medicine catalogue circa 1905.

But aspirin? No. Not even paracetamol. Just a battered bit of plastic and tinfoil with the word "Hedex" perforated by a series of oblong holes showing very clearly that these were now Ex-Hedex.

This was something of a shock. I had always taken a certain pride in the medical kit, having assembled it for the 1988 Singlehanded Transatlantic Race. For this, I had the RYA's *First Aid for Yachtsmen, The Yachtsman's Emergency Handbook* and a gung-ho Australian, would-be yachtsman who also happened to be my dentist.

Together we assembled the wherewithal to perform any medical procedure short of removing my own appendix with the kitchen knife and a shaving mirror.

The dentist had come into the picture after I first approached the doctor: "Could you prescribe something to keep me going if I break a wrist?" I'd asked, reasonably enough.

The theory was that a spinning winch handle seemed about the most serious catastrophe which I might hope to be able to cope with – icebergs and Newfoundland trawlers, I reasoned, were beyond the scope of even more most well-stocked ice cream tub.

The doctor eyed me over the free calendar from the drug

company on the edge of his desk: "I will not have you taking prescription drugs without proper medical supervision," he said.

"But what if I break a wrist or something?"

"Then you take your Paracetamol and remind yourself you're British."

I went to the dentist.

What he gave me then was still in the ice cream tub and unopened six years later when the toothache struck. It had a long name which I could not begin to pronounce and it came in huge, lozenge-shaped tablets which looked as though they might have been prescribed by a French doctor for the other end – or else, it occurred to me, an Australian dentist with a sense of humour. Anyway, I took one and knew nothing until I woke up, recovered but dazed, the following morning.

All of which persuaded Tamsin to tackle the ice cream tubs. As the ship's medical officer and a qualified nurse to boot, she set about the job with a certain alacrity.

There were wound dressings in there that were growing their own penicillin. The scissors were rusted into a brown lump. The cotton wool looked in worse shape than the oily rags I kept for the engine.

But then, as I explained, I hadn't needed the medical kit very much. All the way across the Atlantic, there had only been one real emergency – when I overbalanced while taking a sun sight and, anxious not to damage the sextant, had arrested my fall by wrapping my teeth around the genoa sheet.

There was a certain amount of blood – but nothing you could actually bandage. In fact, I was explaining this on the chat show to a fellow competitor – an American in a Carter 30 some 50 miles astern – when he announced: "No problem, I'm a maxilla-facial surgeon. I've got a full operating kit on board. If you heave to, I can be with you in eight hours. We'll lash the boats together, and I'll wire up your jaw."

I was grateful for the offer – especially as he said he didn't usually make house calls. But considering I had carried the spinnaker all night when he had been down to just a headsail, I was damned if I was heaving to. Besides, I felt as if I could carry on, just as long as I kept off the oatmeal biscuits provided by the very square-jawed competitor from the Royal Marines.

In fact, in all the years and thousands of miles since, virtually all I have needed from the medical kit has been an endless supply of waterproof plasters. Which, I suppose, proves the old Law of Nature; the one which states that in all things – from spare clevis pins to wire cutters – if you have them, you'll never need them.

But run out just once…

It was intriguing to read this 28 years later: Since my conversion away from pharmaceutical products (see the health page on the blog), I no longer carry any drugs – no antibiotics… not so much as an aspirin. Just lots and lots of waterproof plasters.

Chapter 34
All Aboard for a New Life

This was the first instalment for the Daily Telegraph on January 2nd, 1995.

This year is going to be different. I have resigned from my magnificently important-sounding post of chief correspondent of the London *Evening Standard*. I have closed my expense account, handed back the company car, I have turned over my flat to a Japanese corporate tenant, and I am setting out, at the age of 45, to find a new life.

Everyone should have a new life sometime, and this is mine. I have worked for it. I have dreamed about it, and it starts now.

It begins with a voyage around Britain in a small boat going very slowly. With me will be Tamsin Rawlins, who has shared my life for the past three years and who, as a school nurse, has had quite enough of grazed knees and sick notes. Also, there will be Blue, a sort of Labrador who has no idea of the length of the walk coming his way.

We have sold all our possessions except for those we can carry with us, or which can be stored away in a cardboard box in an attic. We have worked out a budget which requires an income one-seventh of the one we had before, and we shall earn it as we may, knowing that when funds are low, we can economise or move somewhere cheaper – like the Pacific.

The main point of it all is that we shall have time – time for those things which ought to come free but which turn out to be far too inconvenient to fit into the maelstrom of career and city life.

Time, for instance, to decide on those Sunday nights when the sun comes out just at the end of a typically dreadful British weekend, that we are not going to clamber onto the motorway and fight our way back to London along with all those other people who have to be in the office on Monday morning.

Instead, we will sit in the last of the evening sun and watch as the harbour is reclaimed by the swans and the returning fishing boats, and we will raise a glass and wallow in our good fortune.

And Monday itself may find us nosing up a tiny creek or

anchored in some secluded bay while we prove to ourselves that the British summer really does have just as many glorious days as it did in our childhood – and once again, we will be there to make the most of them.

Even in winter, there will be a two-hour walk every day with coastal paths and country pubs to discover and small ports where we will stay for as long as we like or until the weather lets us move on. When people in other boats set out in gales or take to the train, we will hug the smugness to ourselves and wonder why we did not think of this sooner.

In fact, we thought of it earlier than most. There is a little-known but well-established routine in which retired couples take to the water, wrap their savings in a sailing yacht and arrange for the pension to be forwarded to banks around the world.

But we have no pension. In fact, we consider that, rather than retiring, we are just starting out in life – and this is what seems to cause the confusion. People look earnestly into our faces for signs of lunacy. They ask: "Is this wise?"

Wise? We never wondered whether it was wise. It was good. It was worthwhile. It was a dream we both cherished... but "Wise"? We could counter that only with the old saying: "He who lives without folly is not as wise as he thinks."

Of course, this did nothing to dissuade most people from the view that we were indeed mad. For a start, there was the business of disposing of the old life. A year ago, we had two flats and a mountain of possessions which any two people might accumulate over a combined 75 years. It took 10 months of car boot sales to shift everything. Heaven knows how anyone managed before car boot sales. Every weekend found us setting up our two trestle tables and clothes rail on a patch of waste ground in London's Crouch End where the clientele can be divided roughly into those who haggle over the last 10p on an ancient frying pan and those who buy £15 of collected poetry without a murmur.

We made £250 on the first day. We were ecstatic. At this rate, it would take no time at all to raise the £5,000 we had calculated would see us through the first six months. As a reward for our efforts, we blew a good chunk of the profits on lunch at the local Italian restaurant.

Later, the threshold was lowered, and we had to make £100 to earn lunch – but by that time, the best had been sold.

Sometimes we agonised over how little we could expect for what had once been treasured possessions (Tamsin's red silk suit went for £25. My set of Russian dolls with the face of Marilyn Monroe, just £10). We had to remind ourselves that *things* did not matter. It was the way of life they were buying that counted.

By the time the clothes rail was decimated, and the Conwy Pottery had gone for £3, I was ready for the moment when the *Evening Standard* gave me back all my old cuttings – trays and trays full of bursting brown envelopes. Ceremoniously, I threw the lot into the wastepaper bin. One by one, concerned colleagues retrieved reports from China and Czechoslovakia.

"You can't throw these away," they said. "This is a lifetime's work."

Ah, but a different life. A life not wanted on voyage.

So, what are we taking with us? Well, there was always the problem of the books. We started out with some 2,500 and now are down the four boxes – not much more than 100 – half in store until we can get through the rest.

Of course, there are some permanently resident in the ship's library: Chamber's Dictionary (essential from Scrabble players) Delia Smith, Robert Louis Stevenson, Jonathan Raban...

A guitar, made in Romania, which I might possibly learn to play, nestles next to the water tank and tucked away by the nautical almanac is the daintiest box of watercolours you could wish for.

We have two folding Bickerton bicycles which are no longer made but still the best. We have 200 tape cassettes being rotated like the books and four albums of photographs to fuel the constantly changing exhibition in the cabin. Also, we have a great deal of wine – rather more than we need, actually. I made an unexpected visit to Calais just after the budget, and it seemed sensible to take advantage of the opportunity...

Anyway, we will need it because we have all the food from the

London fridge, the freezer and all the kitchen cupboards – and Tamsin has always been a strict disciple of Lady Thatcher in matters of stand-by ingredients.

Somehow, all of it fitted into the biggest estate car in the hire company's brochure, and now we can look at our boat *Lottie Warren* sitting rather lower in the water than usual and know that she is our home.

At just 27ft long, she is a compact home – but then, we have the entire British coastline for a garden.

Chapter 35
The Next Step

"But what are you going to do all the time?"

It was not a question that had troubled us greatly.

Boredom had never been a problem on the boat. The problem had always been piling back onto the motorway on Sunday evening, particularly when a weekend of gales and rain had miraculously transformed itself into one of those breathtaking sunsets that appear on the Boat Show brochures.

So, we have made a decision. We are not going to go home anymore - and announcing it has produced a barrage of questions.

First of all, we have to explain that we are going to move onto the boat permanently. We are going to embrace the live-aboard lifestyle. And why not? Other people do it – there are enough books on how to do it. In fact, to read Bill and Laurel Cooper, you would think there was some sort of a rush on and that if we didn't book our patch of blue water off the palm-fringed beach soon, someone in a Hallberg Rassy would get there first.

So we made our decision. We decided that what had been a detailed but distant plan was going into action at once – before next summer.

And all out yachtie friends have been thrilled: "You won't regret it," they told us. "If only we had done it sooner," they said. But we found that explaining the logic to everyone else has been a different matter entirely.

For instance, how do you explain to someone who has just wrestled their mortgage down to manageable proportions and is already casting around for a country cottage that you are selling all your books at car boot sales and advertising your clothes in Loot?

"What, all of them?" At this point, people turn to Tamsin for reassurance, "Surely not your lovely red silk suit?"

Very carefully, Tamsin explains the pointlessness of a red silk suit on boat, even though it breaks her heart to see it on the "For Sale" rail with a £25 sticker on the lapel.

Gradually the word gets around: John and Tamsin are going to live on a boat

"Oh really, where?"

Well, we're not actually going to be anywhere in particular. We're going to be sort of cruising around.

So, somebody comes up to me in the corridor, prods me in the chest and says: "Ah, so you're the chap who's going off to sail round the world?"

Well, not actually round the world - not as such, not to start with. At first, we'll just be going round Britain.

There is a pause. The questioner digests the reasons why anyone should choose Britain instead of The World. Apparently, it is the equivalent of Cunard announcing the next cruise of the QEII will be calling at Clacton-on-Sea, Barry Island and Morecambe Sands.

Then they ask how long it will take.

About two years.

"Two years! But you can sail round Britain in a month, can't you?"

Well, yes, technically you can, but…oh, never mind.

How do you explain to someone the delights of going slowly – of waking up on a weekday morning in a deserted creek and having breakfast in the cockpit while the water runs away - and goes on running away as if someone somewhere has pulled out an enormous plug. Until, eventually, there is just the occasional rivulet where the curlews strut and peck … and the only sound is that peculiar sort of crackling that comes from drying mud? And what sort of explanation can there be for expecting to spend an entire summer making our way through the French canals – so that we will be lucky to reach Spain by the winter?

The next question is inevitable: "Then, how long are you going to be away, exactly?"

Well, sort of indefinitely, really. We haven't thought about it. We're just going, that's all.

"Just going?"

Yes.

This is when they give us the odd look - the look reserved for the intellectually challenged. It is clear that people do not "just go" – at least, not people who are this much past their gap year. There is the inference in that look of irresponsibility, of foolishness and everything else up to impending doom.

And yes, it is possible that it might all go wrong. Maybe we will get bored. Maybe we won't be able to earn a living. Maybe the confines of a small boat will indeed pressure-cook the relationship until one of us gives way to that irresistible temptation to throw the other over the side.

But then again, things can go just as wrong without ever leaving home.

So, in the end, we are left with Tamsin's sister Judith and her question: "But what will you do all the time?"

She has heard the tales of previous cruises. She has seen the photographs taken in the Brittany sunshine and she can guess a good deal. So she says: "I suppose you'll just have nice breakfasts and drink wine."

Well, not all the time…

Chapter 36
Horsey Island

It was the bank that started the trouble – one of those new banks on the end of the telephone. I rang them with our new address: Yacht Lottie Warren, care of Ship-to-Shore mail forwarding agency on the south coast...

"Yes, we are living on a boat .... yes, it is very exciting. Well, first of all, we're going to sail around Britain.

And what happened? The first statement arrived addressed to "Cottage Warren".

But can we expect anyone to take us seriously? Although we may have cut our ties with the land in the sense that we no longer have jobs, cars or council tax demands, there is a problem in that the voyage itself has yet to begin.

It is, after all, mid-winter, and for three weeks, the gas fitter has been working on the boat's heater. Under these circumstances, only the most intrepid would venture further than the end of wire connecting the dockside electricity point to a tiny fan heater in the cabin.

Ship-to-Shore forwarded the post in packages fastened with bright yellow tape, with a logo showing an envelope winging its way to a yacht anchored off a tropical island. And where are we? We are in the Essex seaside resort of Walton-on-Naze where the postcards show pale young women clutching beach balls and where you can get roast beef, Yorkshire pudding, three vegetables and two kinds of potatoes for £2.60. It is not, let's face it, exotic.

However, we have found there is an island here. It may not have palm trees. It may consist more of mud than golden sand, but Horsey Island and its owner Joe Backhouse are nothing if not different.

Both of them are at the end of a three-quarter-mile causeway passable for only two hours either side of low tide. Even then, you have to walk slowly, pushing your boots through six inches of pale brown goo. Then a track winds past rusted farm implements and diesel engine blocks in the way the drive of a grander estate might be studded with classical statues.

Horsey Island, which you can visit strictly by invitation only, is not grand – but it is exotic. It has been owned by the Backhouse family since before the second world war and none of them much cared for modern comforts. We knocked – a little tentatively and with clean shoes in a rucksack – only to be informed that boots were welcome in the kitchen. On looking around, it occurred that boots would not have been out of place in bed.

Here the philosophy of basic living has been elevated to the status of a minor religion. From the ten unmatched chairs around the table, nine people and a dog looked up with expressions of mild curiosity. Another dog snoozed in an armchair. A third sniffed something on the floor and left it. A small grey hen perched on the windowsill and stared with one unblinking black eye.

It was not the sort of farmhouse kitchen they have in the magazines. There was an Aga, certainly, but none of the matching pottery that goes with it – just the detritus of a well-to-do squat or particularly rebellious student living.

On his island, Joe Backhouse has established a sort of commune dedicated in roughly equal parts to providing an escape from the rat race for a wide and unusual circle of friends, conserving some varieties of wildfowl and shooting others and breeding Arab horses which Arab princes come a very long way to buy – and not taking any of it too seriously.

At 41, in saggy, unbuttoned trousers and a holed pullover with the label sticking up in sympathy with his uncombed hair, he waved across the remains of lunch for somebody to remove enough dogs from chairs for us to sit down.

Joanna Booth, who spends her week in London as a business-development consultant for Sotheby's, wrestled with the Aga to produce coffee while her husband, James, fretted about taking his rather good gun to the local teal again.

There was a girl called Rusty from Northumberland and another called Vicky from Australia. Vicky had looked after Joe's mother until she died and now looks after Joe with all the devotion that might be expected from the most macho Queensland ocker.

A clockwork crab waded through the crumbs on the table, and

Chris Foot made an effort to introduce himself politely. This was complicated by Joe announcing that Chris's middle name was "Boring" – the reason being that Chris had a job. Apart from Joanna, nobody else laid claim to one. In fact Chris has been on the island for two years and was about to leave for Africa with the Overseas Development Agency.

There was some talk about the work on the island involving English Nature and more talk about the effort involved in avoiding the Arthur Ransome Society, which keeps wanting to come and experience the real *Secret Water* – but mostly it seemed to be an ongoing party. People drifted out as Joe explained about never seeing the need for heating and only turning on the generator during the hours of daylight for rugby internationals on television.

Then he hauled himself up and wandered off to throw handfuls of corn to the guinea fowl, the Australian woodcock, the golden pheasant and the rest.

We went with him and kept walking through the muddy puddles to the causeway where Chris, the boring one, was coming back in the Land Rover. He was, of course, not boring at all. He stopped and leaned on his window as people do when they have time to talk. "It's an incredible place," he said. "Like a sort of private club."

Then he added: "It's different if you live here. It's a hard life."

When we got back to the boat and washed the mud off our boots, the gas man had the heater roaring. It made us feel just slightly spoilt – but, on the other hand, we really will be setting off any day now.

Chapter 37
Watts, Amps, and Angst

We are thinking of naming the boat Sizewell B. With two wind generators and 125 watts of solar panels, on a good day, *Lottie Warren* could earn her keep supplying the National Grid – but that is what happens when you surrender yourself to Ohm's Law.

I once subscribed to the theory – well, more of a religion really – of the KISS principle: Keep It Simple, Stupid. This fundamental truth had been passed down through all the generations of sailing heroes, but simplicity thrives best in the sunshine. Start fitting out a boat for the British winter, decide to make her both a home and an office, and suddenly the fixtures start climbing the evolutionary scale faster than Dr Frankenstein's laboratory mice.

We wanted heat in every cabin, including the head – so that meant forced air … which would need one amp. The computer takes another 1.4, the fridge at least 1.3 … the tape player, the gas detector – all those lights…

Sometimes I wake up in the night and find myself doing mental arithmetic

But that's progress for you. It started the first time I spent a night on a boat of my own. She was on the small side and very basic, but she did have a 12volt battery and two fluorescent strip lights in the cabin - and surprisingly cosy they made it, too – what with the spaghetti Bolognese bubbling on the stove and the transistor radio playing *Friday Night Is Music Night*.

I remember sitting there towards the end of a bottle of wine and thinking what a lovely boat she would be to live aboard. That was how naïve I was then, or at least, how drunk.

Anyway, since I could not possibly destroy the moment by going to bed, I was still sitting there with a silly grin on my face when it dawned on me that the cabin no longer seemed quite so cheery. Indeed, it was beginning to look decidedly gloomy. In fact, it was getting downright dark.

The battery was dying.

There was, of course, nothing to be done about it but to go to bed. There was no way of charging the battery apart from taking it home and plugging it into the mains. That was the year the outboard acquired an alternator, and I lost my innocence.

Since then, like virtually every other yachtsman, I have become a slave to electricity and the means of generating it. The trouble with this is that once there is a theoretically unlimited supply, I start to find all kinds of different ways of using it.

Yachting magazines do not help. Nor do boat shows. It takes a purist of the utmost determination to turn his back on electronic autopilots and digital logs and maximum average speeds, not to mention the joys of Muscadet that is colder than the bilges.

As so the boat fills up with wire. There is an interesting correlation between the yachtie with a new electronic toy and the child on Christmas morning: suddenly, it becomes far more important to see the thing working than to read the instructions.

This means that the electrical system on a boat can become somewhat idiosyncratic, and once she has been through two or three owners, it graduates to the totally incomprehensible.

How often does the temporary installation "just to try it out" or "until I get around to buying a 5amp fuse" still turn out to be in situ five years later? Besides, the whole electrical system was only temporary – dating as it did from the original owner who had bought a job lot of red wire, which meant you could never tell positive from negative without a multimeter or blowing yourself up.

That was why I always felt so guilty showing prospective buyers around. I could cheerfully punch a button, point to the obediently illuminated display and never get round to mentioning that the whole thing only worked because I had tapped into the nearest point in the lighting circuit, and then only with the help of a reel of plastic adhesive tape.

When the surveyor came to look over her, his recommendations included: "A qualified electrician should be engaged to tidy up the electrics.

He was right, of course – just as I am sure I am right to bring in an expert to turn *Lottie* from a basic weekend cruiser into a floating power station. Now I have regulators and dump resistors and current and capacity monitors and something called a buzz board, which sounds like high-level corporate gossip. The march of progress seems to have achieved a momentum all of its own.

It didn't stop until the qualified electrician had this idea that there would be such a huge electrical surplus that we ought to install an immersion heater.

But I still have a recurring nightmare that I will wake up and hanker after paraffin lamps, a drip-fed diesel heater and an old Olivetti.

———————

Chapter 38
The Pint Pot

To the designer, it is the cockpit - a place of cunning helmsmanship, conscientious watchkeeping, furious winching and sometimes, lunch.

To us, it is the cupboard under the stairs.

You can tell the difference as soon as you lift the flap of the canopy: Instead of neatly coiled sheets, winch handles in their pockets, serious-looking arrays of instruments, all you can see are cardboard boxes. We have just become liveaboards, and our belongings are living here.

We knew this was not supposed to happen. We had read all the books and knew everything there was to know about a measured countdown to the eventual pushing off. We cannot even blame the unexpected opportunity to go three months ahead of schedule: The fact is we have just brought too much stuff.

To be perfectly honest, we do not need 100 books – and I'm not talking about *Macmillan's* and the *Sight Reduction Tables*, but John Mortimer and Paul Theroux, William Bond and Iris Murdoch. And who needs all that underwear?

We have enough underwear between us to stock a busy Knightsbridge boutique. They never tell you this in *Sell Up & Sail*, but once you have sold all your winter coats and ballgowns, you are left with your underwear and no one wants that – at least, no one wants mine. Also, there is the argument that one day, you will require more, it would be foolish to throw it away now. Instead, you stick it in a plastic bag and say: "Don't worry, we'll find somewhere for it."

Result: a cockpit full of underwear.

And toiletries. We never realised it, but both of us seem to suffer from a little-known psychiatric disorder which compels us to buy toiletries at every opportunity. With me it is toothbrushes and toothpaste – I'm always convinced I'm about to run out, and so, every time I pass Boots, some unseen force drags at my ankles, and there I am with a bag full of plaque-attack and incomprehensible chemical formulae.

Tamsin has a similar problem with soap. She thinks she is buying it to give to friends. She is wrong. Meanwhile, we may not be able to get at the bilge pump, but we will go down smelling very sweetly.

The wine is something else. With considerable precision, we had stocked the bilges, then laid in enough at home to see us through until the day we had set for departure – and then one of my last professional assignments took me to Calais. What was I to do? It is as easy to get out of Calais without a bootful of plonk as it is to come away from the Boat Show without a plastic bag bursting with brochures.

And so, moving the case of slightly suspect Corbières, which happened to have a very nice picture on the label, we come to the tools.

Well, I thought we were going to reach the tools. I took them home to mend the bicycle before advertising it in the free-ads paper. They must be around here somewhere…

But that, of course, is the trouble with the cupboard under the stairs. You start throwing things into it as soon as you move in and continue throwing things into it until the day you move out.

I once left a house with a removals van half-filled with stuff I swear I had never seen before – which duly disappeared into the cupboard under the stairs in the next house.

All of which works perfectly well if you really do have stairs – and a cupboard under them.

If not, you have a problem. We realised this as soon as we planned to set sail, and the mainsheet turned out to be under the box of computer manuals.

Even that might have been manageable without the food. Seasoned yachties will nod knowingly over the problems of stowing the victuals: anyone who has ever embarked on an ocean passage with a full crew knows how difficult it is to find space for two beers a day per person for 40 days – and that is without worrying about the stick of bananas (tie it to the backstay).

But try emptying all your kitchen cupboards, the fridge, the freezer and the fruit bowl and putting that lot in the galley lockers.

So where did it end up?

Don't ask. Anyway, it's all being moved tomorrow. If it stays where it is, nobody is ever going to take us seriously.

We have made a start: I have looked around the boat – from the bow locker, which seems to be full of guitar, to the one under the foot of the double berth which is packed with tapes we forgot we ever recorded.

For the time being, it's going to be the dog's cabin. I always said it was absurd that he should have one to himself. Just as long as we remember to lock away the tin opener…

Chapter 39
Woodbridge

They call the final stretch of the River Deben "Troublesome Reach", but when *Lottie Warren* drifted up to Woodbridge on the last of the evening tide, it seemed that our troubles were all over. For the first time since giving up our jobs, selling all our possessions and setting out to sail round Britain, Tamsin and I knew the great adventure had finally begun.

It was a Tuesday, the sort of brisk, sunny winter's day that arrives unexpectedly to turn the town-bound commuter's thoughts to the injustice of life in general. We just felt smug.

At last, we had left behind the marina in Walton Backwaters – nice enough as marinas go, considering that all marinas bear a distinct resemblance to supermarket car parks. Instead, we were heading for a spot where water gipsies deserve to spend the inhospitable winter months: the foreshore in front of the tide mill at Woodbridge.

The view from our cabin window is the very one they put it on the postcards: with the mill now restored to working order, its white clapboard and red tiles standing out sharply against the clear blue sky. It is the sort of place that sparks a sharp intake of breath every time you see it.

True, life is basic here. There are no floating pontoons and electricity points every five yards. No shower blocks and unlimited hot water, no dockside restaurant with a menu which includes the "catch of the day". But there is much that is more important, and we are not alone in thinking so.

At intervals along this river are boats with people living aboard. You can tell them by the economy-sized gas bottled perched on deck, the rusting bicycles propped against the rigging – the tell-tale wisp of smoke from the chimney stuck up like the one on Popeye's shack. Sometimes, walking along the riverside path, you may catch a glimpse of these boat people in their ragged jerseys, busy doing incomprehensible things with ancient, oily tools.

Well, now we are on the receiving end of the curious stares, enveloped in the camaraderie of those who live on the fringes of society. To one side, on a huge grey air-sea rescue launch are Tony and Lil. He plays guitar professionally when the mood takes him but otherwise repairs faults in electronic instruments that leave other technicians reaching for a new printed circuit board and a large bill. She is a biologist who likes to live with her work. The result is the sort of chaotic existence in which the microscope and the oscilloscope compete for space, and the cat picks its way across the table with a delicacy born of long practice.

On the other side are Dennis and Jane, living aboard their steel motorboat which they continue to build around themselves. At the same time, they educate their eight-year-old daughter Erika at home, for the perfectly understandable reason that she learns more that way.

It was only after we discovered all this in the first few days that we began to compare it to the awkward nod we might have expected from new neighbours had we been moving into a London flat instead of a patch of Suffolk mud.

But then, something else we have moved into is a political controversy: it may be that people have been living on boats on the River Deben ever since Woodbridge made its name as a trading port in the 16th century - but that was before Suffolk County Council and its environmental services department addressed the subject. Four years ago, it sought to establish "tidiness and cleanliness" on the river by introducing 34 different regulations, ranging from requirements for a three-gallon galvanised bucket under the sink to 120 cu ft of cabin space per person.

Anyway, our own patch of mud is apparently sacrosanct since Queen Elizabeth I gave it to the local benefactor, and now it is owned by the boatyard. This, in turn, is run by a man who promises to protect our rights until the spring. After that, we're not worried. We'll be off (and so will he, on his own, impossibly small boat, to the Mediterranean).

In the meantime, we live in Woodbridge just as surely as anyone who has paid the considerable sums demanded by the developer of the Tide Mill granary (where the view is almost as good as ours).

And Woodbridge is a very good place to live. It is the sort of town which has a violin-maker and a notice in the window of the clock-repair shop regretting that they cannot work on 20th century pieces.

Also, it has Richard Lane and his wine bar. Richard is a man with a very large personality – and very loud waistcoats – who describes his wines in terms such as "poor man's burgundy" and "eminently gluggable" and calls his establishment simply "The Wine Bar" rather than anything involving an apostrophe.

His partner, Australian Sally O'Gorman, began with her aunt's recipe for meatloaf and now has a reputation which extends beyond the county boundary.

It was at the Wine Bar that Tamsin first tasted roasted garlic and goat's cheese – and I made the terrible mistake of having something else. On our latest visit for a belated New Year celebration, the triumph was passion fruit, orange and cardamom ice cream. You could tell, from the first spoonful, this had not come out of any kind of carton.

We only hope they were not looking the following day when we scuttled past with our dozen bottles of £1.39 Vin de Pays from the supermarket. It would have found no place on The Wine Bar menu, no matter how amusingly described. But it was on special offer … and people who live on budgets on the mud always have to return to reality in the morning.

Editing this for the book 27 years later, it is worth adding a note about what became of little Erika Maude, the home-educated eight-year-old on the motorboat. She turned out to be a talented trombonist. Of course, talent is 90% practice, and we were to spend a winter listening to that practice – after all, the trombone is the loudest instrument in the orchestra. Anyway, Erika earned a music scholarship to Woodbridge School – but also a case of scoliosis, that spinal condition in which the backbone grows out of alignment (the trombone is a lop-sided instrument).

The doctors wanted to insert steel rods alongside her spine as they did with Princess Eugenie, but Jane was no more inclined to follow their advice than she had been to send her daughter to primary school. Instead, she sought out a revolutionary exercise programme developed in Germany and Spain - and, sure enough (with the same tenacity that yielded such spectacular results on the trombone), Erika was able to stand straight again.

But that was not all. At 19, she announced that she would devote her life to ensuring that other sufferers should not have to have their backbones bolted to steel rods either. She went to Spain to learn the techniques, rented an old barn on the outskirts of Woodbridge and established Scoliosis SOS Ltd.

Today it has branches in London, Birmingham, Bristol, Manchester and Dublin, and treats patients from all over the world.

Erika Maude is recognised as one of the leading experts in the non-invasive treatment of spinal conditions.

Scoliosis SOS may be found at www.scoliosissos.com.

Chapter 40
Hot Gossip

Largo had a brick. There are probably not many racing boats which run to a house brick tucked away in a cockpit locker, but a rather opinionated friend had delivered it with such ceremony that I found myself unable to throw the thing away.

That brick did two Atlantic crossings and an Azores and Back – not to mention cruising Brittany, Normandy and the West Country: It was a well-travelled brick considering it never once did what it was supposed to do.

It was supposed to heat the boat. According to the rather opinionated friend, a house brick placed over a gas flame will radiate heat far more efficiently than the flame itself.

Indeed, unlike the flame, a house brick can be wrapped in a towel and placed under the saloon table. The crew may then sit and warm their feet on the brick, and it will still be warm enough, later on, to go in a sleeping bag. A house brick, in other words, was as indispensable to a boat heading for the Grand Banks as a radar reflector or a fatalistic approach to life.

Actually, I never got to use the brick. The North Atlantic that year was unusually warm so I cannot tell you whether the brick-on-the-cooker heater actually worked – much less, whether it is as effective as its distant cousin, the terracotta-flowerpot-on-the-cooker heater.

But then, I am probably not the best judge, having very nearly done away with myself when experimenting with the cooker itself as a boat heater. The logic was infallible: Cooking always made the boat nice and warm, therefore, the obvious way to warm it up after a brisk run up the Swinge in early September was to light the cooker.

The subtle difference is that, when whipping up the spaghetti Bolognese, you do not stretch out on the settee berth between adding the mince and mixing the Oxo for a couple of hours' kip. It was only later, on waking with the mother of all headaches, that I remembered what the science master had said about the process of combustion and the way it consumes oxygen in large quantities, replacing it with various gasses quite useless at supporting life.

After that, I decided a heater was a luxury anyway. It was all very well if you already had a fridge and self-tailing winches and an anchor windlass, but not really necessary for the proper running of the ship. Besides, I rather liked going down to the boat before Easter and putting one sleeping bag inside another and sweeping the snow off the decks in the morning. It made me feel frightfully keen.

Now, however, the heater has assumed an importance previously achieved only by things like the rig and the engine. Those early spring weekends were all very well when I could get back into the car on a Sunday night, turn the knob on the dashboard to the stop at the end of the red sector, and emerge 60 miles down the motorway with the temperature on the inside somewhere up around Florida in a heatwave.

All I can say now is that Monday morning bears a distinctly different aspect when, instead of waking up to the friendly ticking of radiators, the day is heralded by a drip of condensations falling onto the end of your nose and the first thing you see when you open your eyes is your own breath.

So now we have a heater. It was very expensive, terrifyingly sophisticated, and, in the three weeks it has taken to get it working properly, I have thought a good deal about cheaper and simpler alternatives - everything, that is, except the brick.

I recalled spending a school holiday aboard a converted sailing lifeboat in the Oslo Fjord, when the only thing keeping out the onset of a Scandinavian autumn was a cast iron solid fuel stove in the middle of the saloon. It was supposed to run on coke but seemed equally happy with driftwood or even the contents of the gash bucket. It was the sort of stove that should have been surrounded by red-bearded men in oiled sweaters smoking enormous pipes, and you needed a 50ft boat to cart it about.

Then there was a lovely little brass gadget reminiscent of those old shell casings which retired admirals like to keep as doorstops. This one had a chimney on top, and you opened a sort of breech and loaded it with a charge of prepacked charcoal as if you were after the Bismark. It worked splendidly and suffered from only one rather fundamental drawback: The charcoal came in brown paper packets, which tended to get damp and acquire the consistency of a paper bag from a Chinese takeaway just before the sweet and sour hits the carpet. And have you ever seen two pounds of charcoal upended on a settee berth?

Just in time, the thing from the Boat Show worked and proved that progress does have its advantages. If I sit just so, a jet of warm air goes straight up my trouser leg - and you don't get that with a house brick.

Chapter 41
Kent

Summer arrived unexpectedly. You would have thought we would be ready for it after surviving winter with all the stoicism of a pair of early polar explorers. But no, the thermometer's first foray above 70°F found us swaddled in wool and corduroy and beginning to wilt.

The problem was the size of the boat – it was always going to be the size of the boat. *Lottie Warren* is quite simply not big enough for all the clothes required to cope with the full gamut of the British weather, so we had packed away all the shorts and T-shirts and sent them off to Tamsin's parents' attic.

This seemed a good idea for all sorts of reasons. For one thing, only our winter wardrobe would succumb to the damp – and some of it might pass as mildew-coloured anyway. Besides, Eddy and Eira had been rather looking forward to a sort of mystery tour of the British coastline, summoned by phone call: "Can you meet us at so-and-so and bring such-and-such?"

The difficulty lay in finding a rendezvous that was not only suitable for handing over the bin-liner full of warm weather gear but somewhere they might actually be interested in visiting.

When the sun first struck in earnest, we were in Battlesbridge in Essex, as far up the River Crouch as you can get without hitting the bridge, and at the first opportunity, we were due to set off across the Thames Estuary to Kent.

I consulted the man on the next boat about a likely place to stop. The boat was a huge Dutch barge, and the man was the local wildlife warden. His suggestion was Foulness Island: "You'll find a lot of signs saying 'No Landing' but don't worry about them. Just stick to the road, and you'll come to a pub called the George and Dragon where you can still get beer for 60p a pint – that's because nobody's really allowed over there – just the construction workers on army contracts and the like. Tell them the wildlife warden sent you."

We went and looked at the island. It was grey and forbidding with what appeared to be watchtowers where I imagined sentries with searchlights and machine guns kept a lookout for people after a 60p pint. Warning signs – dozens of them in large red letters – insisted that landing was strictly forbidden and added chilling remarks about guard dogs and the Ministry of Defence police.

An invitation from the wildlife warden suddenly seemed less impressive. We pushed on across the estuary to Harty Ferry, somewhere between the Isle of Sheppey and Kent.

But this was not much of a place to invite anyone. There is not really anything on the Kent side of Harty Ferry – not even a ferry anymore. Just a spring where sparkling freshwater gushes out of a sort of parish pump.

A man with a hatchback full of one-gallon plastic cans was busy filling them one by one: "It's good for the plants – much better than the stuff that comes out of the tap. Some people drink it too."

We drank deeply. Put this stuff on a supermarket shelf with a picture of a mountain on the bottle, and you could make your fortune. But there are no mountains at Harty Ferry. Just a sea wall and a muddy creek up to the Shipwright's Arms, a pub renowned for being still unconnected to mains gas, electricity or water.

It makes up for these deficiencies with a good deal of character. There is a nautical library behind the bar, and incomprehensible navigational instruments lie dotted about as if the last customer was an absent-minded admiral.

But it was still not a place you would want to invite anyone for more than a convivial evening. We pored over the chart. Whitstable only accepted yachts in emergencies. Was excessive body heat an emergency under the harbour regulations? Ramsgate was out because they have a bye-law prohibiting dogs afloat or ashore within the Royal Harbour limits.

I rang them, suggested this was absurd, said we could prove the dog had been nowhere near the Continent. They refused to budge.

And that was how we came to Sandwich. Like many of the happiest choices in life, it was reached by a mixture of desperation and convenience. Not that it mattered. Finally dressed for the weather, we sat looking out at the town quay and realised that, quite by chance, we were at the heart of one of England's most picturesque medieval towns.

To one side was the ancient toll bridge – actually, we hit the ancient toll bridge in our enthusiasm to arrive. It still has a scale of charges posted on the wall: "Every chariot, landau, berlin, chaise, chair, calash or other vehicle drawn by six or more horses or other beasts 2/3d."

Nothing, apparently, about poorly-handled sailing boats.

We walked around the 14th century town walls, pausing every few yards at boards depicting the sort of varied scenes befitting a Cinque Port and – before the river silted up – Britain's foremost trading harbour.

One way and another, Sandwich does not let any scrap of history go unrecorded. As well as the bed where Henry VII slept and the field where Henry V's longbowmen practised before Agincourt, there is a plaque on the wall of the minicab office commemorating the day in 1922 when Sandwich's Mayor declared open the East Kent Road Car Company.

It came as a natural progression to call at Strands Tea Shop and find a notice outside saying that the proprietor had spent "a short period of time as cook/housekeeper to the Princess Royal".

Actually, Connie Hussey's royal connection lasted just a month – but who's counting?

Chapter 42
An Inspector Calls

The Animal Health Inspector chose his words with all the care of an Old Bailey Judge in the days when they still kept a black cap under the bench.

"What we are talking about," he said, "is six months quarantine. We are talking about having the dog destroyed."

Admittedly, the dog was not helping much. Ever since *Lottie Warren* sailed up the river to Rye, Blue had been looking forward to his run ashore. The Romney Marsh is home to 20 per cent of the entire English sheep population, and there is still something in his rather complicated genes which tells him lambs just want to have fun.

So, when the Animal Health Inspector came and enquired about the dog aboard the vessel, Blue hopped onto the quay, wagged his tail and sniffed the visitor appreciatively.

The Animal Health Inspector's face registered alarm: "Please, the dog must not come ashore until I have verified the facts."

Oh, very well. I called softly, and Blue sauntered back by way of a small boy carrying an ice cream at dog level. The Inspector swallowed hard.

These were the anti-rabies regulations in full force, but we never expected to meet them head-on in Rye, a lovely little town immortalised as "Tilling" in the Lucia novels by E.F. Benson. From these books, we knew it as an "ancient and enlightened town", and Tamsin had been reading hard in preparation.

So hard, in fact, that she had acquired something of the personality of Lucia herself, whose relations with petty officialdom bring to mind the phrase "withering scorn".

It was all my fault, really. I was the one who had filled in the harbourmaster's form about an animal aboard, and then mentioned by way of conversation that, from Dover, we had made a quick trip across the Channel to fill up with wine and had left the dog with the kindly man in the marina office. His own dog had died last year, and he had been reduced to going round to his mother to play with hers.

None of which the Animal Health Inspector believed for a

moment. The dog, he ordered, was to be confined to the boat while he went off to telephone for verification.

This was becoming needlessly complicated. The harbourmaster's form had never even asked if we had been to the Continent with or without a dog. If I hadn't mentioned it, nobody would have been any the wiser – and besides, if we were going to lie about it, surely the first lie would be to say we had never been out of the country.

Meanwhile, the best of the day was being wasted. Quite apart from any walking, we would soon be too late to book a table for dinner at the Landgate Bistro.

So, when the Inspector returned and said that he had been unable to contact anyone and now required the animal to be confined below decks until further notice, there occurred what the court might describe as "an altercation". We refused. The dog needed a walk, and he was going to get a walk. He had broken no law. He was a free dog.

"Are you aware of the anti-rabies regulations?" demanded the Inspector.

Of course, we were. Why did he think we had left the animal in Dover?

It was at this point that Lucia entered the fray and called the Inspector: "You Stupid Man".

"Six months quarantine," replied the man. "The dog destroyed," he added for extra menace.

"Only if you can prove he's been abroad," I retorted.

At this point, a salient fact emerged: It appeared that the man – stupid or otherwise – had tried only one of the two phone numbers we had given him to verify my story. But we will never know how this might have influenced events because, at that moment, the dog decided to reassert his starring role in the drama. Seeing the Inspector about to walk off in the direction of the phone box – or possibly, the sheep-filled fields of Sussex – Blue jumped back onto the quay.

Or, at least, he jumped halfway. The Inspector caught him in a sort of headlock just as his back paws left the boat – but before the front ones connected with the quay.

The result was something like a Tom & Jerry cartoon where the dog remains suspended in mid-air, all four feet scrabbling at nothingness, and there is an agonising second or two when you know he is going to drop off the bottom of the screen.

It was not quite what happened in this instance. Instead, Tamsin leapt to the rescue and gave a final push which should have enabled Blue to scramble to safety. However, the Inspector, his mind still reeling with images of anti-rabies posters, pushed the other way. The fact that the dog did not end up in the water can only be attributed to his own powers of levitation.

After this, Tamsin had to stand outside the bistro and calm herself by reading aloud about leek and Roquefort tarte and steamed fillet of wild salmon with chive hollandaise.

She was still there when the Inspector returned, having finally verified what we had been telling him all along. With monumental awkwardness and mumbled assurances that we could each see the other's point of view, we shook hands. I am sure it made us both proud to be British.

Chapter 43
Walking the Plank

You can tell a lot about a boat by her gangplank. In the Med, where they call it a passerelle, it can have a tasteful blue awning, a balustrade and wheels on one end. In which case, the yacht attached to it is likely to have satellite communication, a Mercedes in a locker under the sun deck and somebody in a white coat holding a silver tray of champagne.

Our gangplank is not like that. Ours is more of a plank. It has a slot cut in one end to fit around the base of the pulpit, a bit of rope to hold it there, and one of the dog's discarded towels underneath to protect the gelcoat.

But I am as pleased about it as if it had come complete with a Royal Marines Band to play on the quayside each time I stride up it. Well, not so much stride as sidle – having waited to see if it will bear first the dog's weight and then Tamsin's. Actually, it bends horribly and makes me think of the wording on the boatyard contract, which says it is used at my own risk.

But none of that can take away the pride and sense of occasion I get from having a gangplank. I mean, would the Duke of Edinburgh have looked half as distinguished in his uniform of Admiral of the Fleet if he had had to get off Brittannia by cocking his leg over the guardrails? Would he be seen picking his way across the decks of half a dozen destroyers before scaling a seaweed-covered ladder up the harbour wall to emerge on all fours at the feet of a family in Kiss Me Quick hats eating chips?

Certainly not; His Royal Highness has a gangplank – or in his case, a "brow".

But I am not sure whether he ever had the problems that go with it. For one thing, there is the dog. A dog on a boat quickly comes to realise that his territory is bounded by the guardrails, in much the same way as his garden is bordered by the hedge. But take down one section of guardrail, give him ten feet of gangplank, and it is the equivalent of opening the garden gate.

To begin with, Blue was content with the inboard end. He sat there rather in the manner of a security guard. I suspect he had a clipboard somewhere. After a while, he took to positioning himself in the exact centre. This made him look like a contestant in one of the sillier events in the town regatta.

This might have been endearing but led to all sorts of trouble when he discovered that it was but a short step from the middle of the gangplank to the quayside - and no distance at all to the bench where people sat to eat their sandwiches.

It was after our third expedition to retrieve him that we began to think that maybe the gangplank was not such a good idea after all – at least not without some means of hoisting it up or swinging it inboard at will - because the other thing to remember about a gangplank is that it represents power.

Look what happened to Woodgates when he made the mistake of accepting a week's flotilla racing in Greece. Arriving in the typically picturesque harbour, the skipper moored alongside a large wooden ketch flying the Australian flag – the sort of boat with acres of brass and varnish that ends up on all the postcards. The flotilla crew duly stepped across onto the gleaming teak decks, filed down the passerelle – pausing to admire the Turk's heads on the handrail – and wandered off in search of lunch.

Returning sometime later, full of dolmades and retsina, they were understandably miffed to discover the Australian had withdrawn his passerelle and had apparently disappeared, which of course, was impossible since the passerelle was neatly stowed, meaning he has to be aboard.

After a good deal of hailing, he appeared in the companionway and announced that no, he would not be putting it out again for their benefit. He was fed up with people tramping all over his decks. To his way of thinking, if people wanted to get ashore, they should make their own arrangements. And yes, it was a matter of supreme indifference to him if people ended up being stranded through their own foolishness.

After such a good lunch, the flotilla crew felt the afternoon was turning into something of a disappointment. Nobody would lend them a dinghy. The harbourmaster had gone home for his siesta. The fishermen were out fishing. It was not until the evening sun bathed the town with that golden light typical of the Greek islands that the Australian mellowed too and allowed his neighbours back aboard – extracting abject apologies with every step.

He is probably still there, still peering through his brass portholes, looking for likely victims.

And the awful thing is that I know exactly how he feels.

Chapter 44
Holidays

We are just back from our holidays – yes, thank you, we had a lovely time; very relaxing.

Just because we have given up our jobs, moved onto a boat and set out on what can only be described as the "pursuit of pleasure", we do not have to forego holidays.

When summer arrived, we too, experienced that ingrained instinct to get away somewhere --- anywhere. We looked at the chart and realised that, without compromising the object of this cruise around the country, we could take in the Channel Islands. They are, after all, a part of the British Isles but, also, they are considered to be *different*.

We began to realise just how different when we were still three miles off the island of Alderney. This is the nearest, but it is still 13 hours' sailing from the mainland. And, you will remember, we have a dog – a dog that would have to clear customs before being allowed ashore for the first opportunity to cock his leg since Poole.

I called Alderney Harbour on VHF and outlined, as tastefully as I was able, the predicament. We did not want a repeat of the Unpleasantness in Rye.

By contrast, Alderney's customs officer agreed to meet us at the yacht club. We could buy him a pint. Yes, Alderney is different, all right - just walking around the place is different: we packed the rucksack with fresh bread and brie, peaches and a cold bottle of rosé and set out to explore.

There is a walk around Alderney for wimps, which goes on roads and tracks. We, on the other hand, stumbled through rabbit paths which disappeared into the gorse, up inclines from which we lurched, gasping onto cliffs and ultimately, we came to Telegraph Bay.

If this existed on the mainland, some council official would have issued a bylaw to close it and put a barrier across the top. Here there is just a sign that says: "Dangerous steps. Use at your own risk".

It did not say how dangerous. We counted 186 rough steps before this descent of 250ft imposed a total commitment to survival. When the track merged with a stream and the mud slid beneath our feet and left us clinging to exposed roots with our fingernails, we assumed things could only get easier.

They did. There was a rope.

There was also a precipice. At the bottom, unsurprisingly, there was no one else - which was what made it so essential to get there in the first place.

Sark is not like that. In Sark, the steep paths to the bays are carefully maintained. This is because the place is so rugged that there is no other way to reach the sea. Clambering up from the anchorage, we came to a monument in memory of a party that set out in a sailing gig in 1868 and were lost in a squall which arose with "heavy rain and thick darkness". The inscription urged upon others "caution and warning".

Possibly, this was why we kept disappearing from Sark - dashing back to Guernsey at the first hint of bad weather. Sark has charm, with no cars, its horse-drawn carts and tractor-drawn fire engine, but Guernsey has something even more appealing and totally unexpected: In Guernsey, there is a tradition that just about everybody sells their surplus garden produce.

Given the amount of sunshine they get, there is always a surplus of garden produce. Every day, we walked around the lanes, darting back and forth between the little wooden hutches perched on stone walls and filled with lettuces and radishes, spring onions and raspberries – all at a fraction of the price in the shops. Our greatest find was four huge figs laid out on a fig leaf and costing £1 – which we were invited to slide down a plastic drainpipe into a milk churn half-filled with water as a precaution against theft.

By the time we reached Jersey, we had come rather to accept that we were in a foreign country. It has its own money, its own stamps, and heaven knows whose way of pronouncing place names. Also, five minutes after arriving in the picturesque harbour of Gorey, the phone rang with a call from the very last person I expected to hear from an old colleague at London's *Evening Standard*.

It was a hot afternoon in London, he said. Everyone in the office was fed up and looking forward to going on holiday, and the talk had turned to the one who had gone on holiday for life.

It was an odd sensation, really, sitting in the cockpit, watching the afternoon sun cut shadows across the fort on the hill, listening to the gossip which had once seemed so important.

In a few days, we would be returning to England – back to work. Only, in our case, it was a return to a routine which dictates that, somewhere in the week, we find an hour for me to open up the little computer and write something - while Tamsin passes on orders for her *Going to Boarding School* book.

No wonder we needed a holiday.

Chapter 45
Life of Luxury

As the owner of a luxury yacht, I would like to make one thing clear: The mildew at the back of the knicker locker is going to be dealt with just as soon as I get around to sewing a new bit of yellow cloth onto the end of the frayed burgee.

For those readers who imagine luxury yachts do not suffer such indignities, I should add that *Lottie Warren* will only qualify as a luxury yacht if she sinks in some spectacular fashion – possibly involving the Navy and certainly lots of helicopters.

Then, the newspapers will recount that we have gone missing aboard our "luxury yacht".

You know the sort of thing: "Two Britons were feared drowned today after their luxury yacht was reported missing in gale force winds and mountainous waves…etc…etc…

Why is it that nobody ever goes missing aboard a modest family cruising boat?

Well, for one thing, it is not nearly as interesting and anyway – apart from the occasional "Captain Calamity" who sets off from Skegness in a converted trawler, navigating with the AA road map and has to be pulled off every sandbank in the Thames Estuary, most yachtsmen do not fall into a media niche. We do it for fun, and we spend more on our hobby than people do on gardening or darts. Obviously, we have "luxury yachts".

There is absolutely no point in telling the man from the Daily Gabble that there is a steady leak in the deck join at the chainplates, the engine smells of hot diesel because you crossed the threads on the injectors, and the cooker is inoperable on starboard tack because there's an apple down the back and you're waiting for it to rot and ooze out by itself.

If you try to explain all this, you will merely make your mark in the cuttings library as an eccentric with a luxury yacht: "Despite owning a luxury yacht, he attempted to play down his vast wealth…"

We know all about this since Tamsin, in the marina laundry in mid-winter, found herself being asked: "Are you on holiday or are you just rich?"

She says she never really replied. She was sorting socks at the time, and you would have thought that that would be answer enough.

So, what exactly should constitute a luxury yacht? If we can get this sorted out, we can issue a set of guidelines to the press and save a lot of embarrassment all round.

My own view is that a luxury yacht has a crew. Indeed, it has a skipper in white ducks and someone with a silver tray and an ingratiating smile. Tamsin insists the inventory should include a dishwasher and an airing cupboard. It tells her she's not trying. She thinks again and comes up with a walk-in refrigerator and a spin-dryer.

Since we started on this, we find we have a ready basis for dreaming up impossible luxuries without compromising our principles – an icemaker built into the cockpit, hot water – you can imagine the sort of thing…

Also, a luxury yacht should have the name picked out in gold leaf on a plaque on the side of the coachroof. She should have a full set of signal flags and someone to get up and scrub the teak decks early in the morning so that by breakfast time, they have dried white and hard and gleam in the tropical sun.

The luxury yacht should have an ancient Scottish engineer called McTavish hidden away in the forepeak. He should wear slightly soiled white overalls and carry a small canvas toolbag. Whenever I attempt to mend something and inexplicably wreck it beyond all hope of repair, McTavish will appear with his tap set and wooden-handled screwdrivers and say something like: "Och Sorr, is the wee drive shaft oot o' alignment, then?" Then he will set to, whistling soft Highland melodies and rescue the situation.

There should be a boarding ladder that sticks out sideways so you can walk down it like stairs, and at the bottom, a varnished launch so large that you get into it by stepping on the gunwale, without it tipping upside down.

And on board the luxury yacht, nobody ever, ever says: "I thought you made the dinghy fast. I couldn't do it because I had the shopping/dog/water-can (which anyway, is still empty because we couldn't find the tap)" And even if they did, there would always be another dinghy in which to go and collect the first.

It would all be so different, and yes, it would all be so dull - which is why people with real luxury yachts always look so miserable.

And that is the end of the fantasy for today. If you will excuse me, I have to go and take the furling gear off the forestay for the third time in a week. Please don't ask me why.

Chapter 46
Beaulieu

Somewhere there is a tropical island with my name on it. There is white sand on the beach and clear blue water in the lagoon – and fresh green coconuts tasting of champagne. But that is not the vision that has been preoccupying me lately.

This voyage round Britain, if it proves anything at all, is supposed to prove that there is a paradise on our doorstep – and the other day, we found it.

Actually, we knew it was there. This was not one of those occasions when a routine stop or an idle detour reveals an unexpected gem. This time we had made ourselves an appointment with the tranquillity of the upper reaches of the Beaulieu River.

It was certainly the most compelling reason for visiting the Solent at a time when the preparations for Cowes Week make this 25-mile stretch of water so crowded as to be almost impassable to all but the most determined yachtsman. Huge sailing machines doing terrifying speeds buzzed us like multicoloured birds of prey, swooping out of the middle distance, their crews in matching strips as if they were soccer teams.

We nodded politely and edged out of the way, not entirely sure that going so fast was making them any happier. They ignored us, intent on the work in hand.

But then, it would have been quite inappropriate to arrive in the Beaulieu at anything more than the most leisurely pace. The first time we ventured further than the marina at Buckler's hard had been in a tiny inflatable dinghy with a sail fixed precariously on top. It was just as well that as the evening advanced, the wind died away.

But we had a bottle of wine with us and no shortage of time and drifted up on the tide beyond the last of the moored boats. There, the New Forest closes in around the water, shutting out the notion that anything should need to be done in a hurry.

Indeed, we drifted so slowly that at times the swans overtook us and led us round a bend in the river to a tiny pool where a single boat lay at anchor. On deck sat a solitary man with his face tilted to the evening sun and a glass resting on his knee.

As a tiny ripple splashed against his boat, he opened one eye, considered whether we might be a threat to the all-pervading stillness of the moment and then observed: "You look content."

We replied: "So do you," and drifted languidly on our way.

One day, we promised ourselves, we would have a boat of such modest draft that we could anchor in Beaulieu's secret pool.

That was three years ago, and like all the longest-held ambitions, it could so easily have failed to live up to its promise. But, as *Lottie Warren* ghosted past the tightly-packed yachts in the marina and the riverboat disgorging its day-trippers, that long-remembered evening recreated itself right down to the shadows cutting across the lawns of the grand riverside houses and the swans pushing out from the banks to greet us. They might even have been the same swans – at least, we like to think so.

To begin with, we sailed between two lines of moored boats, past private jetties with signs saying, "No Landing". Gradually the size of the boats diminished, and the jetties took on a rustic and neglected air. Long trails of seaweed offered the vague hint that the adventurous were welcome to attempt a landing.

And then we turned the final bend, and the Beaulieu opened out into what can only be likened to the maritime equivalent of a woodland glade. Oak trees screened the houses, a pair of horses wandered down to the bank, curious to inspect the new arrivals. As the splash of the anchor broke the silence, the ripples spread out as if to announce that we had now reached some sort of epicentre of serenity.

We stayed there for almost exactly 24 hours. During that time, one small motorboat puttered up to Beaulieu Abbey, turned round and puttered back again.

Occasionally we saw walkers on a path at the other side of the fields and once, a man on a bicycle. The horses, after a while, grew bored with our presence and wandered back to the far fence where the more serious walkers kept apples in the side pockets of their rucksacks. Down on the river, a pair of swans brought their four cygnets and tapped their beaks on the hull as if demanding rent. It was our only interruption. Even they paddled off as the sun went down behind the trees, and the water turned from gold to purple.

Dinner that night was served in a setting for which, you would expect to have to sit on an aeroplane for several hours – and face a bill that would go a long way to spoiling the whole evening.

But Tamsin gathered fresh basil from the pot that nestles in the centre of the lifebelt and alfalfa from the plastic carton next to the washbasin and set them on the table with fusilli and chorizo sausage in tomato chilli with oregano.

We would not have swapped places with anyone who had managed to get a reservation at the Master Builder's Hotel in Bucklers's Hard.

In the morning, we went to check on this decision. We took the dog and landed at the less rickety of two ancient jetties, walked through the horses' field and along the path to this fastidiously preserved piece of 18th century England. You wouldn't know there was a hotel there at all, just a row of carefully preserved shipwrights cottages with audio-visual presentations about Nelson's navy and parties of schoolchildren losing their clipboards.

We looked at the menu in the glass case and nodded to ourselves. Then we walked home for lunch – back through the woods, across the field, down the rickety jetty; back to that other Beaulieu River, there to lie in the sun undisturbed – until the swans came calling again.

Chapter 47
Mud, Glorious Mud

You can have too much of a good thing – especially mud.

To hear some East Coast yachtsmen go on, you would think that mud was invested with some sort of mystical quality. A couple of chapters of Maurice Griffiths and the visitor from the South Coast begins to wonder how they could have wasted so much of their life stepping ashore onto gleaming hardwood pontoons when they could have been sinking welly-deep into the very soul of the river.

Well, I have a theory about that. I have been working on it for the past year – ever since we moved *Lottie Warren* from the South to the East Coast.

Of course, to begin with, we enthused about the delights of deserted anchorages where the tide went out with greedy sucking noises and the banks advanced at somewhat more than walking pace.

We sat – one particularly memorable Sunday morning – in Landermere Creek, comprehensively marooned by mud and yet perfectly content with the curlews marking their haphazard criss-cross patterns as they pottered about organising their own breakfast. In fact, we sat there for most of the day – until we began to doubt the water would ever return.

For the winter, we moved to Woodbridge and sat in the mud so picturesque that artists flocked to set up their easels at the end of our gangplank.

But now all that seems a long time ago. For one thing, it was before the trouble at Tollesbury.

Also, we still had to learn the Awful Truth about Walton. We were moored snugly behind the Yacht Club, bows to a staging, stern to a buoy, and sitting in the mud for 20 hours out of 24 – or, as we discovered, rather less when the retreating spring tides kept us afloat for barely more than a heartbeat at high water.

We could see ourselves being stuck for a fortnight. We needed to move further out.

On the last day, the instructions for going ashore went like this:

Lower yourself over the bow of the dinghy.

Slide the dinghy across the mud until you can go no further.
Put on the wellies waiting conveniently in last time's footprints.
Wade glutinously to the wall.
Now climb the wall.

It was partly the memory of this, during the three days we spent anchored in Pyefleet Creek, which persuaded us to move each day to East Mersea Point where there is a steeply shelving shingle beach and what the book describes as "clean landing".

And it was my own fault when we returned one evening to find *Lottie Warren* had swung with the tide over an adjacent patch of mud – and not only that but a very much shallower adjacent patch.

This time, we were faced with fully 30 yards of the stuff. It was the kind of mud you had to run through. Lingering on one foot meant sinking up to the knee.

So we ran, pulling the dinghy with the dog in it – which was absurd because he likes nothing better than running through mud. Come to think of it, we should have harnessed the dog to the painter and sat in the dinghy ourselves.

Anyway, all this had to be leading up to something, and the whole sorry business culminated a few days later in Tollesbury, where the book advised landing on a hard on the south bank of the channel. We admired this hard as we sat having lunch in the cockpit.

By then, the time came to go ashore: the falling tide revealed something at the bottom of the hard which was most definitely not hard – an expanse of glistening pale grey…

That was how we came to be motoring around the river looking for another hard – or a harder hard – or the one we had obviously not found the first time.

…until we came to an abrupt and gooey halt and sat and fretted – and were soon, once again, entirely surrounded by mud. We knew quite well what we should have done. We should have become terribly, terribly calm and philosophical.

Instead, I believe there was talk of incompetence, and a door may have been slammed – which is pretty unimpressive given the construction of yacht doors – particularly catamaran doors. Anyway, the upshot was that we concluded we had had quite enough of the

East Coast, thank you very much. "We won't call at St Osyth and the Crouch and the Swale," we announced through gritted teeth. "We'll go directly to the South Coast."

In the end, of course, the tide crept in again and with it a sense of proportion. We skulked back in the dark to where we had started and took a long and therapeutic walk along the sea wall in the moonlight – and, of course, we did call in just about everywhere on the way south.

So one day, we will go back to the East Coast. Again, we will sit and marvel at the tranquillity of a deserted creek as the tide runs out; because by that time, we will surely miss the mud.

I just hope we will be rather better at avoiding direct contact with the stuff.

Chapter 48
Cornwall

We called him "The Viking". He had long blond hair and a flowing beard, and he was looking for crew. In Falmouth, someone is always looking for crew.

The Viking made no bones about this. He had cards pinned up all over town. The older ones said: "Crewgirl wanted" but then he decided people were getting the wrong idea – or, at least, there was a certain absence of nubile volunteers – so he made his quest sexless, at least, on the surface…

Meanwhile, he prowled the pontoons in his singlet, squinting at the sky, ready to leave on the afternoon tide just as soon as someone in very tight shorts and carrying their own toothbrush should come shimmying down the gangplank.

But in Falmouth, there is always rather more expectation than action. This last serious port in England is at once the springboard into the Atlantic and the landfall from it. Arrive here by water, and a sort of ocean-going credibility rubs off.

When we reached Falmouth, it was all: "Where are you from?" and "Where are you bound?" and "What, no baggy-wrinkle?"

And where were we bound? Well, we could hardly say: "South Wales."

So we were going to the Isles of Scilly. You can stay in Falmouth for years saying you're going to the Isles of Scilly, and no one will think the worse of you.

So we stayed in Falmouth and ate pasties. It was impossible to avoid them. From mid-morning onwards, the whole town smells of pasty – and not just any pasty but figgy apple pasty and even, heaven forgive us, chocolate and banana pasty.

People wander along the road eating them, sit on the harbour wall and feed the crusts to the seagulls – or else contemplate the growing pile of pastry crumbs on their boats while deciding not to leave this afternoon after all.

Personally, I consider it an achievement that we reached Mousehole - at least it was on the way to Scilly. But the summer ended abruptly with the arrival of the tail-end of Hurricane Iris.

Mousehole is home to the Penlee Lifeboat. There is a little memorial garden to the entire crew who lost their lives in similar sort of weather in 1981. It was quite enough to persuade us to greet Iris from inside the lock gates at Penzance.

We played a lot of Scrabble, a certain amount of backgammon, listened to shipping forecasts – and ate more pasties. In the middle of all this, we had visitors. One of the lesser-known laws of the sea is that no sooner do you announce your plans than everyone wants to come and stay – all at once.

My younger son, George, came with his friend Toby. Toby was a keen sailor, had a transatlantic voyage to his name, battered deck shoes – the lot. He spent two days playing backgammon and listening to shipping forecasts.

No sooner had they left than my elder son, Olly, arrived. With Olly, we came within an ace of leaving for St Ives, only to have the harbourmaster pin up his four-day forecast. It might just as well have had "STAY PUT" written across it in large red letters.

That we ever rounded Land's End, let alone started on the long haul up the Bristol Channel, is rather more a credit to patience than seamanship or anything to do with getting wet and uncomfortable. But then, we were never in much of a hurry.

The fact is that when all those ocean-going types (except, perhaps for the lonely Viking) were raising the Canaries on the horizon, we slipped into Padstow just as the first lobster went into the pot at the Seafood restaurant.

I would like to be able to report that, after all those pasties, we were there for the dénouement. But such delights come out of the treat fund – and that is in a desperate state just presently. So it had to be a pasty again – albeit, Mr Stein's rather superior fish and tarragon pasty.

All the same, perhaps it is time we moved on from Cornwall – while we can still move at all.

Chapter 49
Shower Power

This is a sneak preview. One day you will be queuing round the block for this - or else you will get it free with the latest Jeffrey Archer and the *Time-Life Book of Fossils:* I have decided to write a bestseller.

Now, I know there are some yachting columnists who think they can make their fortune with a sailing Aga Saga (or, as it should be termed, All-brass Taylor's Tale), but what the reading public really needs is *The Good Shower Guide to the Ports and Harbours of Great Britain.*

The idea hit me the other day like an icy blast. Actually, it was an icy blast. The 50pence worth of hot water had run out after 42 seconds instead of three minutes - or possibly this was my own fault because I had spent two minutes 18 seconds working out how to adjust the temperature control.

Anyway, you know the feeling: Covered in fragrant hair-and-body shower gel, lovingly distilled from the essence of a hitherto undiscovered South American lichen, corrected for pH balance and developed without cruelty to anything – or, to put it another way, soap - I found myself suddenly faced with the usual choices:

I could stay under the sub-zero deluge and try to fight off the heart attack by sheer willpower.

I could drip my way to my trousers, fill the pockets with soap while discovering that I did not, after all, have another 50p piece.

I could dash for the steward wrapped in a towel.

I put my clothes back on and wander stickily but with dignity into the bar.

Or I could just stand there and rage at the injustice of the universe in general.

The point about all this is that I did not need to go ashore for a shower at all. We have a perfectly good shower on the boat.

Well, that is not entirely true – and like many of the happiest accidents in history, it is the reason why this definitive work is being undertaken: *Lottie Warren's* shower is rather unusual.

We tried terribly hard, but there was nowhere we could put a water heater where it would not either melt the headlining, toast the back of the neck of anyone sitting at the saloon table or empty the water tank while heating up 50ft of pipe.

So, instead, we opted for two-thirds of a shower. There is the bit that pumps the water in and the bit that pumps it out. But for the heating element, we rely on a kettle of hot water added to a gallon of cold in a jerry can and then we stick the inlet tube into that. It works rather well.

Oh, all right then, it'll just about do if there are no showers ashore - which is where we came in. It is entirely possible that, by the time Tamsin and I complete our circumnavigation of the country, we will have experienced the best and the worst that marinas, yacht clubs and the municipalities of the UK can offer.

For instance, there is the little unisex chalet on the quayside at Rye where you may luxuriate in unlimited hot water at the ratepayers' expense. The council also provides potted palms, pictures on the wall and a lock on the door – which, believe me, is not to be taken for granted.

Then there is the lady in Weymouth who runs the municipal showers rather in the manner of a cloakroom attendant in one of those elegant but discreet West End hotels: She keeps a visitor's book and remembers boats from one year to the next. Last time we gave her a box of chocolates.

But it would be unfair, at this stage, to name the yacht club maintenance man who started out by explaining that the reason the showers were cold was because this was the first time they had been used this season, and then - when they fired superheated steam across the room - that the boiler took time to settle down.

Then there was the little man I found round the back of another quayside premises with a screwdriver. He was already looking slightly startled after the shriek which accompanied the instantaneous transformation from Gas Board advert to Edwardian prep school.

"Did you do something to make the water go cold? "I demanded with what I thought was great charm and understanding.

"I only," he stammered. "I mean, I just turned this switch here…"

Oh, we'll see them all before we're done: The irritating little buttons you have to lean against or else the water stops every ten seconds, the trough in the middle of the floor where the water gushes up to float off your shoes like a pair of lighters with severed tow lines, the exotic brands of shower gel left by passing crews from Estonia and Poland. The lost socks…

Readers wishing to reserve their copy should send a jam jar full of continental shower tokens that don't seem to fit anything but which have holes drilled in the middle and would make rather good penny washers…

Chapter 50
Watchet

The dog found it first, plunging deep into the thick, purple goo and leaping out in an explosion of filth that covered everyone within shaking distance. The dog, at least, was happy.

When we set off on this adventure, we promised him the longest walk of his life: coastal paths, woodland tracks, crumbling cliffs and rocky promontories – and, of course, beaches. It was the beaches that appealed to Blue.

Because beaches mean birds – and what do birds mean? They mean the wretched dog disappears in completely hopeless pursuit of the entire British seagull population, and I have to run after him. The dog does not learn, but I am becoming extremely fit.

Still, there was the compensation that once we left the Thames estuary, we also left the mud behind. Returning from a walk on the south coast, there was no longer any need for the quayside hose.

So, imagine our relief at witnessing the dog's first glimpse of Camber sands. He stood for an instant at the edge of the dunes as if he had to stop and pinch himself. There, to one side, was a herring-gull convention just getting through the opening remarks while, a little further on, more sanderlings than he could reasonably comprehend ran back and forth like footballers warming up before a match.

And all this on acres of perfectly clean sand. He thundered up and down the shallows, all the while getting cleaner and cleaner. What was more, when we returned to the boat, he retired to his cabin (he has one to himself), and we did not see him again until the next day's gallop.

It had been like this all through the summer. At Ryde, on the Isle of Wight, he was so well exercised we had to take in the straps of his lifejacket. Then his epic walk came to an abrupt and gory halt. He stepped on a shard of glass and came limping back leaving a trail of bloody paw-prints.

What happened next could only have happened in seaside Britain: the harbourmaster alerted the deckchair attendant, the deckchair attendant volunteered his little truck, and we made our mercy dash to the vet squashed into a tiny cab with 50 deckchairs rattling along behind.

Blue recovered, of course. In fact, he became a celebrity; *Country Life* despatched a photographer to the Channel Islands to take his picture. The dog was rapidly taking over. When we arrived in a new port, nobody wanted to know about us. Instead, it was all: "So, this is the famous dog…"

The trouble with all this attention was that it gave him an even more inflated impression of his own importance. He took to lying around on deck all day so that he could be admired by passers-by.

And it was in this frame of mind that he came to what was probably the greatest beach of all, the Doom Bar at Padstow. Every day, Blue ran his marathon on this gigantic sandbank, throwing up rainbows of salt spray and even, from time to time, standing up to his neck in the water and shaking himself – which was even more pointless than chasing seagulls, but what did it matter? He was enjoying himself, and he was clean.

So, I suppose that as we sped with the boiling tides of the Bristol Channel towards Watchet on the Somerset coast, we should have realised that the good times had to end. The water – which had been deep blue and even, on occasion almost turquoise – suddenly turned brown, the colour of mud.

We had forgotten about the mud in Watchet. We only remembered the peculiar pink rock which falls out of the cliffs and lies strewn about the beach – we had taken some back to London and sold it at a car boot sale as doorstops.

But Blue remembered the mud. By the time we had walked into it – and I had lost a gumboot, then my balance and finally plunged my stockinged foot into the stuff, the dog came lolloping by and shook himself all over me - and I swear he grinned. It was as if we were back in Essex, and the whole golden south coast had been nothing but a glorious dream.

———

Chapter 51
Mumbles

It was not Everest. But on the other hand, it was there.

Every day Mumbles taunted us – as magical as Shangri-La and just as unattainable.

Well, maybe not quite as magical. But, since we are now in Swansea, the little resort at the other end of the beach with its pier and its funny name does sound rather charming.

Besides, everyone has heard of Mumbles. I always imagined it being twinning with somewhere like Obergburgl and full of people telling each other to speak up.

But the beach is four miles long, and at this time of year, with a gale blasting the sand across it and the seagulls flying backwards, a walk to the other end is about as appealing as the retreat from Moscow.

Each day we forced ourselves a little further, agreeing through gritted teeth that this was a marvellous beach compared to the last place: At Penarth, we had marched every day for a mile across broken rock and plastic bottles to reach a cliff path which the dog convinced himself was haunted so that he ran all the way back to the boat – and so did we.

But Swansea was exercise on a grand scale, and so it demanded an expedition. We kept walking.

First, we walked to the grave of Swansea Jack. Back in the 1930s, Jack had been the most famous dog in Britain, hardly ever out of the pages of the *Daily Mirror*. Jack was a retriever who made a habit of rescuing people who fell into Swansea Docks. By the time he died, aged seven, he had, as the inscription said, "saved 27 human and two canine lives".

We sat Blue beside the stone and took his picture. We might have been proud parents photographing precocious offspring outside Number 10 – except that Blue is nine already and has shown no inclination to do anything heroic - or even useful. Still, with no sign of Jack's ghost, we pressed on, the three of us: Mumbles or bust.

We were about halfway when we realised that of the great British explorers in whose footsteps we rather fancied we were following, not one seemed to have been five months pregnant. Tamsin looked about her at the desolate landscape with an expression which would not have suited Captain Scott at all. Briskly, she asked for the nearest public convenience.

Well, this being Swansea and not the South Pole, we found one. But for exactly the same reason, it had a notice on the door saying: "Closed due to vandalism." How we came to squeeze the bump through a gap in the railings and end up in the Social Sciences faculty of the University of Wales is really another story, but we did reach Mumbles – and Mumbles rewarded us.

Under a grey sky and with the sand gusting up onto the Esplanade, with fishermen sitting in their cars and watching their rods waggling in the wind, the town possessed a stoically British charm which seemed entirely appropriate.

And, best of all, down by the pier, it offered quite the most magnificent public convenience either of us had ever seen. Hewn out of solid rock, complete with statues and an imposing façade, the pier facilities must have appeared to the Swansea vandals as some sort of stately home and so escaped unscathed.

And the pier was open. This was not surprising considering that the man who runs it has been there for 30 years, doing the job his father did before him all the way back to 1946. His name is Dexter Ford and he looked over his pile of 2p pieces and said: "Those were the days" – which was somehow exactly what we knew he was going to say.

He went on: "In those days, we had the Bristol Queen and the Cardiff Queen stopping here with the people coming from Porthcawl, Ilfracombe and Tenby. We had dodgems and bazooka guns and coconut shies and sideshows all around.

He paused: "Then the Cinema started opening on Sundays, and it's never been the same since."

Easing himself out of the little booth, careful not to set himself on fire with the bottled gas heater, he made way for the third generation – his son Michael – who climbed in with a plate overflowing with baked beans from the Pier Café & Take Away.

Michael Ford had started out as a motor mechanic and found the business grew on him. Pushing out the coins and forking up the beans, he looked set for the next 30 years.

And Mumbles was growing on us too. We preferred it as a frontier town, huddled against the wind and without the summer's lobster-red bodies spilling out of T-shirts and upending ice creams all over the pavement. We allowed ourselves to be blown along the High Street and there, at the top, was Oystermouth Castle standing stark against the lowering sky as it had for close on a thousand years.

It was closed, of course – but not empty. Through the padlocked gate, we could see people with goose-pimples and smocks made from charity shop blankets leaping among the ruins waving battle-axes.

This was heritage on the hoof. Swains Eye, a subdivision of the Dark Ages re-enactment group Regia Angelorum was rehearsing Saxons v. Vikings.

Dan Cooley, the one in the chain mail, had been a student at Swansea University and may be again: "We travel all over the country," he said. "We were at the Battle of Hastings." He meant the one in 1995.

Next year they will be at York for the Jorvik Festival, although (depending on who else turns up) they may have to be Normans or, heaven forbid, peasants.

He would have let us in but, clinking apologetically, he explained: "We can't admit the public. That would screw up our insurance."

Well, if Saxons can defend castles like that, explorers can take the bus back.

Chapter 52
Flying the Flag

With all due ceremony, appropriate prayers and a marine band playing slow marches if I can find one in time, *Lottie Warren's* ensign is being consigned to the quayside rubbish bin. It has seen good service, but it is now, quite honestly, a disgrace to the ship and a disgrace to the nation.

The problem is not so much that these days it measures a good deal less than its original three-quarters of a yard and is sort of squarish since I trimmed the frayed edge and secured the hem with sail repair tape.

Nor is there anything particularly outrageous about the fact that you can put your thumb through it. No, what has sealed the ensign's fate is its colour

This is not a red ensign anymore. This is a faded orange ensign – a national flag the colour of mulligatawny soup. Normally, I would not have worried, but we had just had the sailcover and sprayhood cleaned, and the colours clashed horribly.

I was explaining this the other day when I realised how dreadful it sounded – as if the entire British seafaring tradition from Drake to Lisa Clayton had come down to a matter of décor.

But looking around the backstays and mizzens and ensign staffs in the harbour, I can see the whole gamut from pink to see-through brown complete with mildew spots and exhaust smuts. There are ensigns here which would fail muster on a tramp ship lifeboat in the Malacca Strait – and some which look as if they already have.

It is, apparently, a British malaise. It would never be allowed in the USA – over there, the FBI has men trained to look out for straggly ensigns as the first sign of un-American sympathies. A good American yachtsman always hoists a very large, very clean ensign – but then he grew up starting every school day by saluting "Old Glory".

The Dutch are just as particular - although possibly for different reasons. All summer, you can see them streaming down the Channel in their business-like steel boats at the beginning of copybook circumnavigations – and every one with a magnificent yard and a half of red, white and blue trailing behind.

The astonishing thing is that when they come bowling home with their rust-streaked hulls and blacked baggywrinkle, they still have beautiful clean ensigns. Do they have them packaged off to ports along the way? Do they stock the ship with spares along with the red lead and Stockholm tar? I never like to ask.

The Belgians are rather keen on the new Euro-flag – which can hardly be much of a surprise. Also, I notice they tend to keep a little Belgian bit in the top corner as if they need to remind the rest of us who runs the place.

And then there are the French. In the same way that a Frenchman will cheerfully use his spinnaker sheets as mooring warps and wash his smalls in the pressure cooker, he has a charmingly cavalier attitude to flag etiquette.

When a Frenchman buys a boat, he pops into the chandler as an afterthought to pick up the smallest, cheapest ensign he can find. He then ties it loosely to the backstay where it remains until it flaps to within an inch of its string – which is presumably the cue to go out and buy a bigger boat.

I suspect that it is the French who are to blame for the state of British ensigns. There was once a time when, no sooner did the sun go plop into the Western horizon, than British yachtsmen would emerge as one from their oil-lit cabins for the evening ritual of striking the ensign. It was pleasantly companionable with people lingering on their counters taking the evening air and discussing the prospects for another glorious day tomorrow (as memory insists, they were all glorious days back then.)

Also, I remember that when I reached the age of ten or so, as a special treat, I would be charged with this vital task. I knew that if I messed it up, lost the halyard through the sheave or something, the British Empire would come tumbling down about my ears.

But that was before cynicism and Brussels took over. Gradually, the ensign stayed up for longer and longer – and the tattier it became, the less reason there seemed to be to take it down at all.

Now, however, things will be different. I have a new ensign, a bigger ensign, an ensign that flies from a lovingly-varnished staff and which cost so much I can hardly bear to hoist it on a sunny day for fear of what the ultraviolet rays are doing to the dyes.

It is flying now - proof that this is a British ship and proud to be so.

Which means, I suppose I will have to get a new bit of bunting for the end of the burgee and polish the stainless steel and see to the varnish…

Reading this in 2022, I am ashamed to see that, along with Boris Johnson, I contributed to the drip-feed of anti-Brussels journalism which eventually led to the UK's disastrous decision to leave the EU. What a price for a cheap joke.

―――――

Chapter 53
Swansea

It is one of the facts of life afloat that everyone assumes I must be able to fish.

"Ah well," they say, when I explain that I no longer have a proper job or a regular income – or really much of an income at all – "you can always catch fish".

And I smile and nod and keep quiet about trailing a mackerel line along the south coast and then across to the Channel Islands and finally down to the West Country, periodically upgrading to increasingly garish lures and ever more improbable excuses.

In the end, Tamsin put away her recipes for mackerel pâté and grilled mackerel with gooseberry pickle and baked mackerel with herb stuffing. Instead, she gave me a look that suggested she was thinking kindly of my other qualities (I can, for instance, hum quite pleasantly). Fish, we could buy.

But then we came to Penarth in South Wales at exactly the same moment as the cod. They come in their teeming thousands at this time of year to feed and breed – and leap onto the hooks of the anglers who flock in the same teeming numbers from the valleys of the Rhondda.

In Penarth marina, the serious business is not yachting but fishing. Every day the car park fills up with heavy-set men pulling tackle boxes from the boots of cars. Every night, the charter boats can be heard returning in triumph.

Tamsin began to dream of cod: Cod provençale, cod charlotte, curried cod. I promised to provide the basic ingredient and booked a six-hour expedition.

The boat was called the *Chara*. She had woken us regularly and boasted a "large heated wheelhouse". The fee was £10 – but then, I reasoned, cod in Tesco's is not cheap. Worms, for some reason, never entered into the calculation. Instead, they appeared on the morning of the trip: slapped onto the counter of the fishing tackle shop, wrapped in the pages of the *South Wales Echo* – a living, heaving, most unpleasant colony. That was another £10.

I began to do some arithmetic: Cod at £3.60 a pound… I would have to catch six pounds…

"And you'll need some squid," said the salesman. It came frozen in a box with "calamari" written on the lid. I imagined it deep fried with lemon juice, dangling from the hook like an earring.

I think I must have seemed an odd addition to the fishing party. The rest were factory workers and unemployed miners, men with life-hardened faces who swore cheerfully through their cigarette smoke and whose stubby fingers worked with astonishing delicacy to tie tiny knots in 40lb breaking-strain line.

The record for these waters is a 43lb cod. The boat's record is 32lbs. The skipper emerged in a blast of hot air from his heated wheelhouse with a spare rod. He had long golden hair like a Viking. He was really a motor mechanic, standing in while the owner was away up towards Bristol in another boat.

The men from the Rhondda pulled on successive layers of padded jackets and waterproof trousers. Then they stood at the rail and ate cold steak pies out of the cellophane. With a snarl of supercharged diesel and a belch of black smoke, *The Chara* headed out of the lock on course for the fishing grounds.

I picked up a worm from my *South Wales Echo* packet and began to push it onto the hook. It made me feel brutal, like a hunter. With a sort of brusque kindness, a man with four earrings took it from me and threaded it far up the line. Then he threaded several more behind it. He spent the rest of the week in a factory making what he called metallised paper. But he thought about fishing.

I cast and overran the reel, creating a small and rather neat bird's nest. Danny, the boat's 18-year-old mate, cleared it without a word of reproach. Elsewhere, the fish were biting: a pair of whiting on the bow. Danny plied the net for cod. I caught a whiting. This was fun.

It lasted fully 15 minutes and then, as if someone 150ft beneath us had blown a whistle, it stopped. The boat swung on the tide. The sun went down in liquid reflections of rose and purple. Danny went into the wheelhouse and the signature tune of *Coronation Street* escaped with the heat. Cigarettes dotted the darkness as conversation drained away with the daylight.

The youngest member of the party, 17-year-old Alun Evans, pulled a black balaclava down over his face. There were individual holes for the eyes and mouth. He looked like a terrorist. His father was the one in a Fidel Castro cap with another terrorist's balaclava rolled on top of that. Then it transpired that he was really Alun's stepfather. The boy's real father was up on the bow, dressed in an all-in-one thermal outfit that made him look like a stuffed toy. Everyone said Alun was lucky – he had two "Da's". That's the way it is up in the valleys.

From time to time, the skipper turned down the television, switched on the fish-finder and chased the cod around. He even stayed out for an extra hour, hoping something would turn up. Nothing did.

We chugged back while the lads argued happily about the total weight of the catch and tried to push surplus bait down young Alun's neck. By the time we locked back into the marina, I was two hours late for dinner and brought with me two small whiting which, we worked out, had cost something more than £10 a pound.

But, as I explained at the time, that's not important. The important part, I had learned from the man with four earrings. He said: "We don't really come for the fish. What counts is having a good day out with the boys, see?"

THE END

(… although the story continues in Oldmansailing:
The Good Stuff – Book Two)

Books by the Same Author
Also Available from Amazon

The Good Stuff - Book Two

In this second volume of The Good Stuff, John and Tamsin have a baby on the boat – and then another one. The idyllic lifestyle, sailing where the wind blows them, sitting over a glass of wine as the sun turns the estuary to liquid gold is suddenly more complicated. Where do you find a launderette in the middle of the French countryside? How do you keep to the maintenance schedule with help from a two-year-old?

At least it was good copy. There was Yachting World's Dogwatch column to feed every month and the Daily Telegraph's travel page. Apparently, the readers were captivated by the couple's determination to put a brave face on even the most desperate situation – or maybe they just liked the dog.

Here you will discover how to win third prize in the Tayvallich Regatta one-oar race and what the home counties school nurse said to the Liverpool "Scally". And where else do you think you would find detailed instructions for casting The Curse of the Stones on troublesome neighbours?

"It is, as the editor of Yachting World said at the time – Good Stuff."

Trident

- The future is out of control, and it's happening now.

A new Prime Minister committed to scrapping Britain's nuclear deterrent - a Russian president meddling in other countries' elections and an isolationist in the White House...Does any of this sound familiar?

John Passmore's prescient novel, written in the 1980s and set in what was then the future, suddenly becomes terrifyingly relevant today.

As NATO collapses and Russia looks to the West, the future of the world rests in the hands of a submarine captain, his aged father, an old-fashioned reporter and a government secretary in love with a man who is not what he seems...

"Fast-moving and immensely prescient, there are echoes of the early works of Ken Follett and Frederick Forsyth." - Daily Mail.

Old Man Sailing

- Some dreams take a lifetime

When COVID-19 struck the UK, the government advised the over-70s to "shield" while the country went into Lockdown. One old man went sailing instead. Single-handed and self-isolated, retired journalist John Passmore used the pandemic to achieve an ambition which had eluded him for 60 years. For 3,629 miles, he disappeared into a world of perfect solitude, adventure and adversity – arriving back 42 days later, short of water and with shredded sails to find himself celebrated on national radio as the embodiment of everybody's Lockdown dream. This is his story. It is also a story for anyone who ever thought a dream was unattainable

"A word-of-mouth bestseller" - Yachting Monthly

About the Author

John Passmore is a retired journalist who escaped Lockdown by setting sail alone into the Atlantic. He returned 42 days later, short of water and with tattered sails, to find himself celebrated on national radio as some sort of hero for missing it all.

His book became an instant bestseller (albeit, in Amazon's sailing category).

This was most gratifying for the author because, despite a successful career as a Fleet Street war correspondent, all he really wanted to do was go sailing and write books.

Old Man Sailing is not just a story of his voyage but also an account of a journey through life in pursuit of an elusive dream.

Also thanks to Amazon, he has been able to publish the novel he wrote in the early 1980s and which had been languishing in his attic ever since. Although accepted by the prestigious Laurence Pollinger agency, publishers found its futuristic plot "a little far-fetched" – it featured a British Prime minister intent on scrapping Trident, a Russian president meddling in other countries' elections and an isolationist in the White House.

With Jeremy Corbyn, Vladimir Putin and Donald Trump, suddenly the concept didn't seem so improbably after all – and sure enough, it turned out that the readers liked it.

Passmore lives for most of the time on his boat and writes a blog at www.oldmansailing.com.

Printed in Great Britain
by Amazon